HEROES IN GRAY

by
Samuel W. Sherrill
General Editor

with contributions from members of the
United Daughters of the Confederacy

THE CONFEDERATE
REPRINT COMPANY
☆ ☆ ☆ ☆
WWW.CONFEDERATEREPRINT.COM

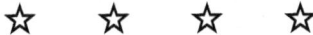

Heroes in Gray
by Samuel W. Sherrill

Originally Published in 1909
by Claude J. Bell
Nashville, Tennessee

Reprint Edition © 2014
The Confederate Reprint Company
Post Office Box 2027
Toccoa, Georgia 30577
www.confederatereprint.com

Cover and Interior Design by
Magnolia Graphic Design
www.magnoliagraphicdesign.com

ISBN-13: 978-692241929
ISBN-10: 0692241922

Contents

Preface

To the children and grandchildren of the men who wore the gray this book is dedicated. It is only right that the children of the Southland know the full meaning of their birthright. No one can object that the truth be told them. It is unjust to the Southland and to those who followed the Stars and Bars to death and to glory not to let the true history of the years 1861 to 1865 be known.

If our children are left in ignorance as to this history they may grow up feeling that they have the blood of traitors in their veins. Nothing will stir the blood of our sons to become true and noble men more than to know the history of such men as Lee, "whose trust was ever in the God of battles," of Jackson who never fought before he prayed, of the Southern woman who nursed the sick soldier, who struggled at home while husbands and fathers fought, who gave their dearest men to the "cause," yet never wavered in their loyalty to it.

We should keep this history before our children so that they may be true to the principle that inspired our heroes — the principle of dying for what they believed to be right. This is the object of this little book.

In the preparation of this book, journals and reliable biographies, and other trustworthy sources have been

5

consulted and freely utilized. Special mention should be made of *The Life of General Forrest*, by Dr. John A. Wyeth. My thanks are due to all who so kindly contributed articles to the book, and to all who in any way assisted in its preparation.

The Author

Introduction

The publication of this work, has been made necessary, by the great demand, in the schools of this country, for short, available sketches of the lives of some of the more prominent men — leaders — who made heroic record, in the days from "Sixty-One to Sixty-Five." This need was keenly felt, in 1907 and 1908, the centennial years of the birth of General Robert E. Lee, the great military chieftain of the South, and now acknowledged, as of world-wide fame, and Jefferson Davis, statesman, scholar and soldier, yet, still more renowned, as President of the Confederate States of America — a Government, which, in its brief life, made glorious defense for constitutional and individual rights, and fell, stainless and pure, on the field of honor.

War is always terrible, and cannot be divested of its accompanying horrors; as conducted by the leaders of the Southern army, it challenges the commendation of all truthful historians, for these made no unnecessary privations and hardships for women and children, by plunder, or destruction of homes. The truth of this assertion is clearly shown in the campaigns of General Lee north of the Potomac, when the strictest orders were issued, and enforced, for the protection of private homes and property, and the historic "crow" need not "have carried his rations on his back" when traveling in the wake of the army of Northern Virginia.

In the sketches now presented to the public in this volume, purposely contributed by different writers, in the interest of truthful and just history, it is sought to give to the student an insight into the character and action of some of the leaders, the chivalry of the South, whose names are now registered high in the temple of fame, who were exemplars of Christian knighthood, who laid down their arms with a sublime acceptance of results and turned to their devastated homes, where, with the great womanhood of the South, a new life, under changed conditions, was carved out, by the "old South," the embodiment of valor, courage and patriotism.

When the re-united country called for followers, in the Spanish-American war, these men, and their sons, sprang to arms with the same loyalty and courage that had marked them in the past, and in them, the "star spangled banner" will ever find devoted defenders. Our service is to our country, our memories are our own — a precious heritage.

Cornelia Branch Stone
President General, U.D.C.
Galveston, Texas

Our Southland

Long time ago the Southern people and their slaves lived on great plantations covering hundreds of acres. These "great-houses," as they were called, had each its own name, such as "Sunnyside," "The Cedars," or "Rosemary." To reach them the traveler must leave the big road and follow the cedar bordered lane leading to the wide, tree-dotted space just in front of the big entrance gate. The house is a stately, white-columned mansion standing on a little eminence, and surrounded by a grove of trees. The front door, with its heavy knocker of brass, is standing hospitably open, with the master of the plantation ready to welcome his guests at the steps. The wide front porch, with its comfortable homemade chairs, is a pleasant place in warm weather, and here breakfast and supper are often served.

As we enter the wide hall, we notice that the floor is made of boards neatly joined by means of small wooden pins, and dark with age and much polish.

The parlor is furnished with many stiff chairs and a sofa covered with black haircloth, so hard and slick that children have great difficulty to keep from slipping off on the floor.

On the walls near the ceiling, are hung portraits of ancestors in red coats, and their ladies in court trains and powdered hair. The ceilings in all the rooms on the first floor are covered with decorations of flowers or fruit done in plaster. The curtains at the small paned windows, and the thick, soft carpet on the floor have been brought on the boat for many miles. There were few railroads in those days and no stores scattered over the country at short distances.

Company Rooms

If the visitors are young ladies, attended by their own colored maids, they are taken up stairs to the guest room with its windows draped in turkey red, and its high mantel-shelf on which stood home-made dips lighted after sun-down. The huge four-post bed is so high from the floor that one must have some little steps to get up to it. Instead of wooden bed-slats, the bed is corded across from side to side with stout cotton cord. On this is laid a straw mattress and then the big, soft feather bed. The whole is covered with snowy linen sheets, and a white, home-woven coverlet. Underneath this large bed is a small, low one called the trundle-bed. This is for the young folks or children and is pushed out of sight and way in the daytime, and pulled out when needed.

If the visitors are young men riding about from plantation to plantation, attended by their Negro body servants, they are quartered during their stay in the "office" where the master has his bookcases and his secretary where he keeps the plantation accounts. This office is a one-storied room somewhat apart from the great house, and is generally built in a lower front corner of the lawn where it has its own separate horse block and entrance.

The Kitchen

The great house never has the kitchen under the same roof. It is always a detached building of much importance. The kitchen floor is sprinkled with fresh, white sand every morning, and this is swept in quaint patterns. Here is the huge, open fire-place on which the colored cooks prepared such good things to eat. Down in the middle of the hot coals sets the iron bake-oven on its stumpy legs. The heavy lid fits close and is shaped to hold coals put upon it to heat the oven overhead. These are replenished as soon as burned out. All the light-bread, sweet potatoes, and puddings are baked in this oven.

In the crisp days when the frost comes the old kitchen is filled with the odor of sage and red pepper pods drying out in the oven. For the year's supply of *fresh* meat must be put away, sausage made and stuffed in long bags, the lard rendered, and the great bowls of cracklings saved for corn-bread.

At meal times the cooked dishes are carried from the kitchen to the dining-room of the great house by processions of shiny-faced piccaninnies, each bearing aloft a bowl or platter. It is the duty of another small, serious darky, with rolled twigs of hair standing out from his head, to mount on a three-legged stool and wave the peacock's feather fly-brush over the table during the meal.

At night the kitchen is lighted by a small, open iron lamp filled with grease. A wick, made of twisted cotton cord is laid in the grease, leaving one end on the rim. This, when lighted, burns slowly but gives a very good light.

Negro Quarters

The Negro quarters are the most interesting part of the plantation. The group of white-washed cabins, each boasting its own patch of garden where the slaves are allowed to raise any vegetables or flowers they liked, is placed at the rear of the great house. These cabins are comfortably furnished, and the slaves are well fed and clothed by their owners. All the time after sundown was theirs to do with as they liked. In these hours they tend their gardens, chop and haul their wood, bottom chairs, and make shuck mats and horse-collars. In these ways, if industrious, the slave make nice sums of money. Some make enough to buy their freedom, while others are set free for some brave act or by the will of their masters. Often these freed Negroes, in their turn, buy and hold slaves of their own color. But these were exceptions.

"Paterrollers"

Each plantation has an overseer, or a man whose duty it is to see that the slaves are employed at some useful work. No slave is allowed to be away from home at night without a pass from his master, else he is in danger of falling into the patrol's hands, or "paterrollers" as the slaves call them. This is a band of Southern white men whose duty was to patrol the country and ride about over the different plantations. If they see a slave away from his home without a pass they arrest him and either take him to jail or else to his master for an explanation.

There was a great distinction of rank among the slaves of long ago. Those Negroes showing special aptitude and brightness are either taught a trade or taken up to the great house. These "house servants" are superior in every way to the "field Negroes," or those who till the soil. The good slave, no matter what his daily toil, has everything to make him contented. If he falls sick, then medicines are provided; if it is a wedding, the bride's dress comes from the great house; or if it is only a "sociable," then the White folks are certain to come for a few minutes just to see how the fun is going. At Christmas is their greatest pleasure time for they are given a week's holiday from work in addition to many presents from their White owners.

The slaves are all very superstitious and believe in signs. If the old rooster crows before the door some morning then it is a sign that company is coming. Or if a red bird flies into the yard then it means something unexpected. They tell the time by the sun; and they plant all growing things in the different changes of the moon.

Home Industries

Many of the articles used on the plantation are made at home by the people there. When you think of the long time it would take for goods to reach their destination in those days of slow travel it is small wonder that the people were compelled to make or raise the articles in most constant use. Candles must be made to light the house, for coal oil and electric lights were unknown.

Tin molds, just the size of a candle, are used; and a twisted cotton cord is run through each mold and tied at the end. Melted tallow is poured into these molds and then left to cool and harden.

Every plantation has its patch of broom-corn of which brooms of all sizes are made by some of the slaves who have been taught the trade.

Most of the medicines were raised in the herb garden or found growing wild in the woods. While the dyes used in coloring the home-woven cloth, carpets, and blankets are made from the bark of trees, walnut hulls, and the juice of the poke berry and love-vine.

The day before a big hunt is spent in molding bullets. Lead is heated until running hot and is poured with due caution into iron bullet molds, a belonging of every home.

Horse collars and door mats were made from corn shucks, while chairs are bottomed with hickory withes, soaked until pliable and then twisted and woven together.

Neither must the shoemaker with his leather apron, his awls, and his wooden pegs be left out of this list.

Spinning and Weaving

The fleecy cotton is the most valuable article possessed by the home worker, and the spinning wheel is the foundation of all home industries. After the cotton has been picked and seeded, it is then carded into rolls. Cotton cards with their sharp little needles tear the cotton apart and clear it of all trash. Then with a twirl of the carder's wrist it falls into the waiting basket a soft, white roll ready for the spinning wheel.

The spinner starts the big wheel going, as she steps back and forth, and spins the roll into thread which is run on broaches or pieces of twisted corn-shuck. If the thread is wanted for stockings or caps then two broaches are wound together, and twisted on the wheel.

Cloth of all kinds from the coarsest home-spun, linsey and jeans to the fancy pattern coverlets for the beds, are home woven on looms worked by the feet. If needed for weaving, the broaches of thread are reeled into hanks, and then run on spools often made of burned-out corn-cobs to find the amount of thread needed before putting it on the loom.

On large plantations spinning, knitting, and weaving go on all the time as great quantities of supplies and clothing are needed by the hundreds of Negroes belonging there. While this work is all done by the slaves, constant care and supervision has to be exercised by the mistress of the great house, or "Old Miss" as she is called by the slaves, to see that the work is properly done.

The Master and His Family

Every morning the master of the plantation has his horse saddled and brought to the door for his daily ride of inspection over the fields. He is accompanied on his rounds by his older boys who help in managing the affairs of the plantation.

The mistress of the home, ably assisted by the daughters, looks after the household affairs, and finds time to pay visits of comfort to any sick slave. The younger boys and girls mount their horses and start to the school-house, which is distant some several miles.

This school, which is known as the Academy, is not free but the parents pay for the tuition of their children.

The house is a plain building, and is not supplied with maps, pictures, and growing plants as are the schools of to-day. The children have to be in their places at eight o'clock each morning, with an hour recess at noon for dinner, which they brought with them; and then "books" again until four o'clock, when they are at liberty to return to their homes. The preacher is generally the teacher, thus combining two good professions.

Amusements

Life is not all work for these Southern people and a picnic or a barn-dance is easily arranged.

The barn-dance is just an outdoor picnic with a basket dinner, and a thick carpet of sawdust spread over the ground for the dancers. The music is furnished by several Negroes, who diligently tune their violins before breaking into the rollicking strains of some well known reel.

A barbecue is on the same order, minus the dancing, but with plenty of fun provided for everybody. The Negro slaves stay up all the preceding night cooking the whole hogs, sheep, and other meats that were slowly roasting in the great fire pits dug in some bit of open ground.

Every plantation had its pack of hounds, and fox hunting is a favorite sport for the men and boys. After the sweet potato crop has been dug and the frost turns the persimmons into balls of sweetness, came the "possum" time.

Camp Meetings

A church, where services are held each Sunday, is in reach of the plantation, and the planter and his household sees that the slaves have special religious teaching in addition to that given them by preachers of their own color.

But it was, and still is, a good old Southern custom to hold an open air camp meeting for one week of each year.

A covered arbor, for the religious services, has

been built in the woods far away from any plantation. This is furnished with plenty of broad low benches and a carpet of clean straw spread over the ground. Around the arbor are built the camps — log cabins without any windows and openings left in place of doors. The cooking is done under a shelter in the background, and the long dining-table is spread on the back porch.

Here in the early fall, families from neighboring plantations would gather to live for a week in the camps, and hold a religious meeting. Relatives, friends, and people from a distance would travel to the encampments; and genuine Southern hospitality is shown by the campers when, at the close of the eleven o'clock sermon, they will publicly invite any and all visitors or strangers to be guests at their camp for dinner or for the length of his stay in their midst.

After the slaves have finished their day's work they hold their meetings a short distance away. The musical talent of those Negro slaves find its expression in religious songs, nearly always sad in character, which they compose themselves. Their singing in the night time, and mellowed by distance, sounds lonely and pathetic.

Causes of the War Between the States

Northern people believed that the States are subordinate to the central government and that the Union could not be broken. Southern people believed that the Constitution is a compact between equal States, and for good reasons the Union may be dissolved.

The North believed that every citizen owes his highest allegiance to the central Government and then to the States, and that the Government has more power and the State less.

The South believed in home duties first, that a citizen's first duty is to his native State, which should have more power given it while the central Government has less.

Abolitionists

There was a class of people who did not believe that slavery is right and that it should be abolished. From this word came their name, Abolitionist. The word "abolition" had been in use before this time, but now took on a new meaning and represented strife and bitterness. With a great number of people the word was a term of reproach and public feeling was against it. But the organization gained strength rapidly, and, as the number of members increased, it was enabled to do material injury to the Southern cause. Its members made speeches, wrote articles for the papers and books on the subject declaring slavery to be a sin and Southern slave-holders cruel and inhuman. These publications caused the Southerners to believe that the people of the North were mean and selfish in trying to destroy the property of others.

The Dred Scott Case

There was a Negro slave in Missouri named Dred Scott whose owner took him to Illinois and then to Minnesota, States in which slavery was forbidden. Afterward going back to his old home in Missouri he committed some offense for which he was whipped. He brought suit against his master claiming to have become a free man by his having lived in the two free States. The Supreme Court of the United States decided that Congress could no more prohibit the carrying of slaves into any State or Territory than it could prevent the taking of any other piece of property. This decision enraged the people of the North who opposed slavery, and they publicly criticized and abused the judges for their decision. This angered the Southern people.

The John Brown Raid

An extreme Abolitionist was John Brown of Ohio who had moved to Kansas, then a Territory, who, with a party of twenty-one men, captured the arsenal at Harper's Ferry. They seized a number of guns to arm the Negro slaves they expected to join them in a war upon the Southern White people for the purpose of abolishing slavery. The Negroes did not join in the undertaking. Virginia and Maryland troops were sent out to the scene; and in the fight thirteen of Brown's men were killed, two escaped, and the rest were captured. The leader with his associates were tried for treason and murder, found guilty, and were hanged.

This raid was so universally approved in the North that Brown's memory is revered there to this day. They regarded him as a Martyr who had been given too severe a punishment for his offense. The Southern people, being the ones he had started out to kill, naturally looked at his action from quite a different view-point.

The Slavery Question

One of the causes leading to the war between the States was the question of slavery. In Colonial times, Northern and Southern people had both believed in slave holding, and Negro slavery flourished in all the colonies and was declared legal by the highest English court of law.

The cold climate and the occupations of the North did not suit the Negro; and slaves proved to be an unprofitable investment. While in the warm climate of the South, and in the raising of cotton, corn, rice, and tobacco the Negro made an excellent servant.

In the North slave labor was finally abolished by all the States lying north of the dividing line run by the old surveyors, Mason and Dixon, between Maryland and Pennsylvania.

Going westward along the Ohio River it was used as a dividing line between the States in which slavery was forbidden and those in which it was allowed. But with the opening up of new territory the dividing line was lost and trouble ensued. Hot disputes were only kept down by forming new "free" States to balance the new "slave" States entering the Union. This compromise was satisfactory to neither party.

The Underground Railway

This was a secret threat to the property rights of Southern slave holders. Away back, as far as 1786, Northern sympathy was with runaway slaves. As time passed this feeling grew stronger until there were certain, well marked out roads from the South to the North which would carry the slave where he was not likely to be found by his master. As the slaves could neither read nor write, this information as to where they could find help and shelter had to reach them by word of mouth. This was a dangerous task for the men who made it their work to slip around from plantation to plantation and make the Negroes dissatisfied.

You must remember that the Southern people had bought and paid for these Negroes, and each one of them represented a large sum of money. They were just as much the property of the man who had bought them as *that* many houses, jewels, or horses would have been. So it is not strange that slave owners objected to the loss of their valuable possessions and always recovered it when possible. A law was made that directed the surrender of fugitive slaves wherever found. But Northern sentiment practically made this law of no use, as assistance in the capture of a fugitive slave was given only when commanded by the Government.

Secession

After the election of Abraham Lincoln as President of the United States, South Carolina withdrew from the Union. In a short time six other slave States — Mississippi, Alabama, Florida, Georgia, Louisiana, and Texas — seceded and took their place by her side. These Southern States believed that when the Northern government allowed its people to aid slaves in seeking freedom that it was a violation of the Constitution. These seceding States declared that as the North had not kept the agreement the South had a perfect right to withdraw from a compact they had voluntarily made with the privilege that any State could withdraw whenever its peace or safety demanded.

The Confederate Government

In February, 1861, a convention of delegates from the seceded States met at Montgomery, Alabama, and formed a new government called the Confederate States of America. Its constitution recognized the rights of each State and guaranteed protection to slavery.

Jefferson Davis, of Mississippi, was elected President, and Alexander H. Stephens, of Georgia, Vice-President.

A few months later the States of Virginia, Arkansas, North Carolina, and Tennessee passed ordinances of secession and joined the Confederacy. The Capital was removed from Montgomery to Richmond, Virginia.

The "Stars and Bars" was adopted as the accepted design for the Confederate flag which floated from the Capitol at Montgomery on March 4th, 1861. Gray was the chosen color for the uniform of the Confederate soldiers, with the colors to denote the branch of service. With the news of secession came the gay, thrilling music of "Dixie," immediately adopted as the national air of the South. This made the tune so unpopular in the North that when the bands played it on the street they were hooted and hissed.

The Aftermath

The men of the Southern army who for four long, hard years had followed the flag of the starry cross through the smoke and flame of desperate battles had now to begin life with empty hands.

Their homes were ruined, their ranks broken by death and their Confederate money of no value. They had shown the world their ability to fight, but they now gave other and better proof of their courage. Hands that had held the sword and musket now handled the hoe and plow.

The army had been filled with men from all classes of society — from the veteran of the Mexican War and the sunburned farmer boy, to the men from the mansions, the owner of hundreds of slaves, fighting shoulder to shoulder with the boys from the mountains. There was no distinction, for one and all fought for a loved cause; and now they again stood equal when all was lost save honor.

Reconstruction Period

The darkest days the South had ever known were close at hand.

For five years the South suffered under the attempts of ignorant men who were trying to adjust the old customs to meet their new laws. This was called the Reconstruction Period.

In addition to the abolishing of slavery, the Negroes were made citizens of the United States with the right to vote.

All public offices were filled with ignorant, dishonest men whose first thought was personal gain.

United States troops were placed in the Southern States to see that these new and bad laws were enforced; and to uphold incompetent officers.

Affairs were in such a bad shape that finally some of the best White men of the South decided to do what they could toward restoring law and order in the Southern States. So they met and organized the Ku Klux Klan, otherwise known as The Invisible Empire or White League. This was a secret society and its members were banded together to protect the weak, the innocent, and the defenseless, and to defend Southern rights and Southern homes.

The time needed the advent of these brave, silent men, wrapped in disguise of snowy white with the three mystic red letters showing what they represented, men who dared exile, imprisonment, and death to benefit the land they loved. Their work was swift and sure, doing more to restore order in the South than any of the authorities.

After the work of the Klan was finished they buried the books containing their objects and rules; and then quietly disbanded. Although thousands of men were members of the Klan not a single disguise was ever penetrated.

The South of Today

The commercial advancement in the South has sprung from the ground, not only in agriculture but also in mining.

Several of the Southern States have their own factories to manufacture cotton goods instead of shipping the raw material away. The marshes and lowlands have been drained and converted into rice fields.

Southern sugar and molasses mills are kept busy in supplying the demand for sweet things. The land has been made fruitful and productive, and the bins and coffers overflow from the results of bountiful harvests. Other Southern States have opened up immense coal mines and discovered quantities of iron ore in unsuspected fields. Wells have been bored and great underground streams of oil have been brought to the surface of the ground in huge fountains. Progress is in evidence everywhere in the South and no longer is the hum and whirr of the spinning wheel or the muffled thunder of the loom heard throughout the land. The Lost Cause is enshrined in the hearts of all true

Southerners, who consider the days of '61 to '65 to be the brightest pages in all the history of the Southland.

Miss Georgia Doty

Dixie: New Version

I wish I was in the land of Cotton,
Cinnamon seed and sandy bottom,
Look away! Look away! Look away!
Dixie Land.

Her scenes shall fade from my memory never,
For Dixie's land, hurrah forever!
Look away! Look away! Look away!
Dixie Land.

CHORUS:
I'll give my life for Dixie,
Away! Away!
In Dixie's land, I'll take my stand
And live and die in Dixie,
Away! Away!

Away down South in Dixie!
By foes be girt and friends forsaken,
The faith of her sons is still unshaken,
Dixie Land!

For Dixie Land and Dixie Nation,
We'll stand and fight the whole creation,
Look away! Look away! Look away!
Dixie Land.

Then up with the flag that leads to glory,
A thousand years 'twill live in story,
Look away! Look away! Look away!
Dixie Land.

The Southerner's pride, the foe man's wonder,
That flag that the Dixie boys marched under,
Look away! Look away! Look away!
Dixie Land.

President Jefferson Davis

In Todd county, Kentucky, June 3, 1808, a little blue-eyed baby was born whose life was to be filled with honors and with tragedy, who was to be loved and venerated by some, hated and vilified by others — Jefferson Davis, President of the Southern Confederacy.

Although born in Kentucky, Jefferson Davis was above all a Mississippian, as his father moved to Mississippi when he, the youngest of ten children, was quite small. When the little fellow was seven years old he was sent one thousand miles on horseback to Kentucky to a Catholic school, where he became the pet.

The boys revolted one day and the priest in whose room the lad slept was the special object of their wrath. They persuaded Jefferson to blow out the holy light in the room one night. When all was quiet he blew out the light, and the boys threw in cabbage, potatoes, biscuits, and all kinds of things. When a light was made and the culprits looked for, all were asleep except tiny Jeff. The priests questioned him severely, and he admitted he knew a little but would not tell. The priest with whom he roomed took him away and talked and threatened

"If you will tell me what little you know, I will let you off," he pleaded.

"Well," said Jefferson, "1 know one thing. I know who blew out the light."

"All right. tell me," eagerly said the priest, thinking he was getting at the bottom of the mischief, and Jefferson said, "I blew it out," and true to his friends then, as in after life, he told nothing else.

His mother longed for her boy, so after a while he returned home, and there he attended Jefferson College for several years. Then he went to Kentucky to the Transylvania College at Lexington, at that time the foremost educational institution west of the Alleghanies. There he remained until just before graduation, when, through the influence of his brother, Joseph, he received an appointment to West Point Military Academy and went there at once. He and his friends expected the examination to be searching, especially in arithmetic, and he dreaded it, as he had no time for preparation. But they had their worry needlessly, as the professor asked a few questions, got started on a favorite topic and concluded; Cadet Davis passed an excellent examination. Mr. Davis was always devoted to West Point, and years afterwards, when he was the great Secretary of War, he made it the equal of any military school in the world. His associates there were Albert Sydney Johnston, Robert E. Lee, Leonidas Polk, Joseph E. Johnston, and others who became famous in the great war. To all of his friends there and at Transylvania College he was always staunchly true. There was scarcely one in his class whom he failed to render some service or promote when he was connected with the United States Government or during the short life of the Southern Confederacy.

At West Point, Cadet Davis was distinguished for his high-toned and manly character, though he did not take a high place in his classes. He was slender and over six feet tall, but had a soldierly bearing and a "springy" step. He had bright blue eyes and high cheek bones. His presence and manner showed a youth of self-respect, determination, and great fearlessness.

One day the class was being taught in a room full of explosives how to make fire-balls. One became ignited. Cadet Davis saw it first and quietly said to the professor, "This fire-ball is on fire, sir. What shall I do with it?"

"Run for your lives," cried the professor, and ran for his.

Cadet Davis did not run but picked up the fire-ball and threw it out of the window, thus saving the building and many lives.

Cadet Davis' father died in 1824, but his oldest brother Joe was always like a father to him, and through his wealth made possible Mr. Davis's brilliant political and public life.

Mr. Joseph Davis, a successful lawyer and large planter, was reputed to be a citizen of great wealth, and this was always at the command of his young brother Jefferson. Mr. Davis was devoted to his mother, and while at West Point sent her each month a good portion of his small pay as a cadet, the first money he had ever earned.

No finer horseman than Jefferson Davis ever lived. He believed a horse and saddle necessary for a commanding officer, and when Secretary of War ordered all his generals to learn to ride. Noticing only a few officers in the army were good riders, he issued this somewhat sarcastic order: "A liberal reward will be paid to any officer or private in the army who will offer a satisfactory device for keeping soldiers from falling out of their saddles. Communications to the Secretary of War will be considered confidential."

*   *   *   *

His distinguished presence in the saddle as well as his bravery in war won him his lovely bride, Miss Knox Taylor, daughter of Colonel (afterwards President) Zachary Taylor, in spite of her father's opposition. Their courtship was romantic, for they met way out in the Indian frontier, where Lieutenant Davis and his commander, Colonel Taylor, were during the Black Hawk War. Colonel Taylor had his family there with him, and the two young people soon formed an attachment for one another, and Lieutenant Davis asked of her father her hand in marriage.

"I have none but the kindliest feeling and warmest admiration for you," said Colonel Taylor, "but I am opposed to my daughter marrying a soldier. A soldier's wife has many trials, and my wife and daughter have complained bitterly of my constant absence from home and their torturing anxieties for my safety, until I once resolved, Knox should never marry a soldier."

The attachment between Colonel Taylor and Davis continued until a court-martial was held. The court was composed of Taylor, Smith, Davis, and another Lieutenant. By the rules of the army every officer sitting in a court-martial must appear in full uniform. The Lieutenant had left his uniform at Jefferson Barracks near St. Louis and had none to wear, so he was excused from appearing. This left only three to vote in the court-martial. Colonel Taylor voted "No," Smith "Yes," and Davis voted with Smith. There was a bitter feud between Taylor and Smith, and Colonel Taylor was furious over Lieutenant Davis' vote. He swore in a forcible manner, "No man who votes with Tom Smith shall marry my daughter," and he forbade Lieutenant Davis to enter his quarters.

The engagement between the young people was not broken, however, and two years later, when Lieutenant Davis resigned from the army, they were married in Kentucky at the home of Miss Taylor's aunt.

The two men did not become friends again until during the Mexican War when both won much fame. The young bride did not live to see this reconciliation, as she died within a few months after going to her Mississippi home, "Brierfield," a valuable plantation which was given Mr. Davis by his brother Joseph for Mr. Davis' interest in his father's Negroes.

Mr. Davis was once defeated for the office of Governor of Mississippi in a remarkable campaign. As in this case, often the real greatness of men is shown in defeat. Mr. Davis' ability and statesmanship were at once revealed, his popularity was unbounded, and ever thereafter he was the acknowledged political leader of his State.

*　　*　　*　　*

When war was declared with Mexico in 1846, Mr. Davis was in Washington a member of Congress. The First Mississippi Rifles, a regiment organized at Vicksburg, elected him their Colonel and asked him to take command. He gladly accepted that position, but declined a Brigadier-Generalship offered him by President Polk, because he was for States-Rights and believed all appointments for volunteer troops should be made by State authorities.

Before leaving Washington, Mr. Davis secured for his men the Whitney rifles, a new and improved gun, which, from being used first by the Mississippians, have since been known as the "Mississippi Rifles."

In the Mexican War not General Zachary Taylor himself won greater renown for intrepid courage and brilliant generalship than did Jefferson Davis. At Buena Vista when the battle was going against the Americans, and many distinguished officers had fallen, Colonel Davis rode forward, examined the position of the Mexicans, and, deciding to attack, brought his Mississippians forward at the double-quick. "Their deadly aim and wild enthusiasm was irresistible. The Mexicans fled in confusion and Davis seized their commanding position. He next charged upon a regiment of cavalry and compelled it to fly with the loss of their leader. Immediately afterwards, a brigade of lancers, one thousand strong, were seen approaching at a gallop, with sounding bugles and fluttering pennons. It was an appalling spectacle, but not a man flinched from his position. Conscious that the eye of the army was upon them, that the honor of Mississippi was at stake, and knowing that if they gave way or were ridden down, the unprotected batteries in the rear, upon which the fortunes of the day depended, would be captured, each man resolved to die in his place sooner than retreat. They stood motionless as marble," under Colonel Davis' low command of, "Steady, Mississippians, steady."

Impressed with their bravery, the lancers advanced more carefully, but were caught within the lines of Colonel Davis' celebrated "V," and were exposed to a terrible converging fire. The fire of the Mississippians was deadly, and the brilliant lancers "recoiled and retreated, paralyzed and dismayed." General Taylor said, "Napoleon never had a Marshall who behaved more superbly than did Colonel Davis today."

On his return from Mexico, "covered with glory,"

honors were showered upon him by towns and cities. Senator Speight dying, the Governor of Mississippi appointed him to a seat in the United States Senate. This action of the Governor was endorsed by the people, and the next Legislature unanimously elected Mr. Davis to fill out the term expiring March, 1851.

Mr. Davis' Senatorial career was a brilliant one. Many intellectual giants graced the Senate during his service, but in ripe scholarship, wide and accurate information on all subjects coming before the body, native ability, readiness as a debater, true oratory, and stainless character, Jefferson Davis stood in the very front rank, and did as much to influence legislation and leave his mark on the Senate and the country as any other man who served in his day.

When a member of the lower house of Congress, John Quincy Adams used to take the measure of new members when they made their first speeches. He would sit near, watch them and listen attentively if the speech pleased him, but if not he left quickly. When Mr. Davis first spoke in the House, the ex-President took a seat nearby while Mr. Davis spoke and never moved. At the close of the speech Mr. Adams went to some friends and said, "Mind me, gentlemen, that young man is no ordinary man. He will make his mark."

In March, 1853, President Franklin Pierce appointed Mr. Davis Secretary of War. Even his opponents admitted his fitness for the position. His guarantees were his West Point training, his long service in the regular army, and his distinguished career in Mexico. His fitness for this new position was soon shown. He was one of the greatest, if not the greatest, Secretary of War the United States has ever had. Under his direction the service was

revised, new tactics introduced, and the infantry provided
with the most improved rifles. Among his innovations
were a medical corps and the minnie ball. The actual
strength of the army was increased, and he secured larger
pay for the men. He planned and built larger and stronger
fortresses at important points, and in their distribution did
not give more to the South than to the other sections of
the country. During the first year of Mr. Davis' Secretary-
ship the War Department was instructed with new duties
by Congress, and the annex to the Capitol was planned
and built under his direction. "Cabin John Bridge," at that
time the longest single arch in the world, was his work.
This is the bridge near Washington from which by order of
a vindictive official Mr. Davis' name as Secretary of War
was erased when he became President of the Confederacy.
The space remains blank, attracting attention and questions from visitors.

*   *   *   *

After four years service Mr. Davis retired with un-
stained hands and with his ability and efficiency acknowledged by friend and foe. He at once resumed his place in
the Senate, to which he had been re-elected in 1856, and
for three years Jefferson Davis, Stephen A. Douglas, and
William H. Seward were the most influential members of
the Senate.

Jefferson Davis was pre-eminently the champion of
the South, her civilization, her rights, and her honor. The
ideal Senator in dignity and courtesy, he was always the
gentleman, and his polished and distinguished manner
made him "the ornament of the highest school of oratory
and statesmanship of his country." He was the champion

of "States' Rights," and was opposed to the policy of Douglas, and his greatest speech was in opposition to "Squatter Sovereignty." One of the most brilliant debates between the two was when Mr. Davis, without previous notice, took the place of his absent colleague and for several hours maintained a running debate with Mr. Douglas.

The next summer he spent in Maine, and while at Portland and on his journey back to Washington he was shown the highest marks of courtesy and esteem. While many in the North and East did not agree politically with the great Mississippian, still they valued him highly and were proud of his able and fearless services for the Nation, both in war and in peace.

At this time by request he made a speech in Faneuil Hall in Boston, where he was introduced by Caleb Cushing and received most enthusiastically. Afterwards at the Democratic Convention in Charleston, in 1860, the votes of Massachusetts were given more than a hundred times to Jefferson Davis for nominee of the Democratic party for President of the United States. A brilliant soldier and statesman, and irreproachable in private life, his unblemished character for personal integrity would have made him a strong candidate in the North, and he was the strongest in the South.

Mr. Davis loved the Union and strove to prevent its dissolution, but he believed his "Sovereign State" had the constitutional right of secession, and when she exercised it on January 9, 1861, he followed her. By nine o'clock on the morning he took leave of the Senate there was scarcely standing room in the galleries; sofas and pass ways were full, ladies sat on the floor near the walls. The Senators could scarcely get to their seats. When Mr. Davis arose to address the Senate — the last time he was ever to appear before that body — there was profound silence and every eye was turned upon him. At first low and faltering, his voice soon rang out melodiously clear and trumpet-like throughout the chamber. Unshed tears and pathos and a plea for peace were in every tone, and when he took his seat there was scarcely a dry eye in the house.

This speech should be read by every Southerner, and I give a few extracts to show the tenor of it:

"It is known to Senators who have served with me here, that I have for many years advocated, as an essential attribute of State sovereignty, the right of a State to secede from the Union. Therefore, if I had not believed there was justifiable cause; if I had thought that Mississippi was acting without sufficient provocation, or without an existing necessity, I should still, under my theory of the Government, because of my allegiance to the State of which I am a citizen, have been bound by her action. I, however, may be permitted to say that I do think she has justifiable cause and I approve of her act. I conferred with her people before that act was taken, counseled them then that if the state of things which they apprehended should exist when the Convention met, they should take the action which they have now adopted. Then Senators, we recur to the compact which binds us together, we recur to the principles upon which our Government was founded; and when you deny to us the right to withdraw from a Government which thus perverted threatens to be destructive of our rights, we but tread in the path of our ancestors when we proclaim our independence, and take the hazard. This is done not in hostility to others, not to injure any section of the country, and not even for our own pecuniary benefit; but from the high and solemn motive of defending and protecting the rights we inherited, and which it is our sacred duty to transmit unshorn to our children.

"I find in myself, perhaps, a type of the general feeling of my constituents towards yours. I am sure I feel no hostility to you, Senators from the North. I am sure there is not one of you, whatever sharp discussion there may have been between us, to whom I cannot now say, in the presence of my God, I wish you well; and such I am sure, is the feeling of the people whom I represent towards those whom you represent. I therefore feel that I best express their desire, when I say I hope, and they hope, for peaceful relations with you, though we must part. They may be mutually beneficial to us in the future, as they have been in the past, if you so will it. The reverse may bring disaster on every portion of the country; and if you will have it thus, we will invoke the God of our fathers, who delivered them from the power of the lion, to protect us from the ravages of the hour; and thus, putting our trust in God, and in our own firm hearts and strong arms, we will vindicate the right as best we may."

*   *   *   *

Returning to Mississippi Mr. Davis was offered and promptly accepted the position of Major-General and Commander-in-Chief of the volunteer forces of the State. He did not want war and was willing to make any sacrifice for peace, but he believed in preparing for the worst. But a place in the army was not to be his, for the Provisional Congress at Montgomery unanimously elected him President of the Confederate States, a position he neither sought nor desired, but he bowed to the will of the people.

The simple inaugural ceremony was held at Montgomery, February 18, 1861, and consisted of administering the oath of office and the address of President Davis, which was a clear and able defense of the Confederate cause. It was listened to by a large and enthusiastic audience. In the following November after the adoption of the Constitution he was elected President for a term of six years, and the inauguration took place February 22, 1862, at the new Capitol, Richmond.

"The White House of the Confederacy" was his residence, and every honor, every courtesy was shown him. His habits were simple and he surrounded himself with no forms and ceremonies, the humblest citizen being able to secure an audience with him.

While General Lee was encamped near Richmond, President Davis frequently rode out to headquarters, generally alone, never with an orderly. One night, however, he unexpectedly had an armed escort. It was after dark when he left General Lee's tent, and as he rode along a young fellow of sixteen in a gray jacket, a rifle on his shoulder and a revolver in his belt, joined him, saying cheerily:

"Good evening. Is your name Jefferson Davis?"

"Yes; what of it?"

"I just thought I'd ride with you."

"Why aren't you with your command asked the President. Abashed the boy hung his head and said, "I thought you ought not to be riding around by yourself. It aint right with so many bad men about."

The young soldier had made himself the beloved President's bodyguard, ready to defend him and die for him, and rode with the President until near Richmond, then happily returned to camp.

In Richmond President Davis was to know sorrow and care; joy over the many wonderful victories of his armies, distress over defeats and losses and his inability to alleviate the sorrow and distress of others. He was an incessant worker and gave his personal attention to all departments of the service, and did every thing that ability and zeal could do to promote the success of the Confederate cause, yet he has been blamed for every mistake made; failures in battle, decrease in value of currency, want of arms and scarcity of food. No man has been more criticized and vilified than Jefferson Davis, and even some in the South cast poisoned darts and forgot that he took charge of a country without a government, without a currency, without an army, with no navy and no arms, and no factories and armories to make them.

One Sunday morning in 1865 while sitting in his pew in St. Paul's Church, Richmond, President Davis received General Lee's telegram that Richmond and Petersburg would be evacuated that night. This pew occupied by him and his family during their residence in Richmond, is now marked with a brass plate stating it had been his pew. It is just below the beautiful stained glass window, a memorial to President Davis. On the opposite side of the church is General Lee's pew.

Upon the evacuation of Richmond, President Davis and his cabinet established headquarters of the Government at Danville. There he received the news of Appomattox. In all his disappointment and distress he bore himself grandly. He still hoped to strike an effectual blow with Johnston's army, then at Greensborough, North Carolina. But Johnston and Beauregard thought the wisest course, on account of the slender resources of the country and the demoralized condition of the army since Lee's surrender, was to make the best terms possible with General Sherman. So President Davis continued to move southward with the intention of crossing the Mississippi River and rallying all his forces there and continue the struggle. But President Lincoln was assassinated and the North, insanely angry, charged President Davis with complicity in the crime and offered a reward of $100,000 for his capture. So Federal troops were on the lookout for him and he was arrested in Southern Georgia.

Many slanderous, malicious things were said about Mr. Davis' flight and arrest. He, while traveling with his family, was arrested by Federal soldiers and escorted to Fortress Monroe. The soldiers testified that he was the same dignified gentleman, fearless and composed, when arrested as he ever was.

Fortress Monroe is the strongest fortification in the country. There he was placed in cell Number 2, specially fitted up with heavy iron bars across the windows and all openings. From the steamer *Clyde,* under heavy guard and under the supervision of General Halleck and Mr. Dana of the War Department, the fallen President of the late Confederacy was transferred to the fortress. Between lines of blue soldiers the procession moved, first Mr. Davis, pale and haggard, yet calm and proud, dressed in a plain suit of Confederate gray with a gray slouched hat, General Nelson A. Miles holding his arm; they entered, the heavy doors clanged upon them, and the man who had had armies at his command, the ruler of a great country and of a devoted people and who, when the great Secretary of War, had been received there with salvos of artillery and the salute of soldiers, was now a political prisoner. He was charged with treason and complicity in assassination. Two years he spent there subjected to many indignities.

The greatest attraction about Fortress Monroe is that Jefferson Davis was once a prisoner within those massive walls. On a recent visit there the guides pointed out to me the cell in which "President Davis" was kept. I could but think of the terrible scene enacted there May 23, 1865, when this feeble man, with every opening and every window barred and guarded, with sentries in the adjoining cells separated from his only by iron bars so he could be seen every moment, and with two soldiers in the very cell with him, yet irons were placed upon his ankles.

* * * *

Mr. Davis protested against this monstrous order of General Miles and resisted the soldiers, hoping they would kill him and he would thus escape this degradation. But he was overcome and held by four stalwart soldiers while the brawny blacksmith riveted the shackles on one ankle and the padlock locked on the other ankle.

On account of his health and through the intercession of Doctor Craven, the attending physician, the fetters were worn only five days, and instead of the coarse prison fare unfit for a sick, nervous man, meals were sent him from Doctor Craven's house. No knife or fork, only a spoon, was allowed, and the food was cut up before sent. The officials claimed they were afraid Mr. Davis would commit suicide. Waking or sleeping he was never alone a moment, the soldiers in his cell being changed every two hours. A bright light burned in his cell all night so his slightest movement could be seen. No one was allowed to speak to him except Doctor Craven. Think of the torture this refined, cultured man endured from this close watching! Everything he touched, spoons, napkins, and so on, were seized as souvenirs by the soldiers and sent to their sweethearts, and when allowed under guard to walk on the ramparts, men and women gathered around and stared at him until to escape it he would return to his cell.

In all his trials and humiliations Mr. Davis was sustained by an unfaltering faith in an All Wise God. He was a consistent and devout member of the Episcopal Church, and in his imprisonment his Bible and his prayer-book were his only solace and were seldom out of his hand when alone. His prison physician, Doctor Craven, says, "There was no affectation of devoutness or asceticism. Every opportunity I had of seeing him convinced me more deeply of his sincere religious convictions. There were moments while speaking on religious subjects in which Mr. Davis impressed me more than any professor of Christianity I ever heard. There was a vital earnestness in his discourse, a clear, almost passionate grasp in his faith, and a belief that consoled his deep sorrows."

In after life he never alluded to his cruel treatment while imprisoned; he was too manly, too proud, and too brave. He had a heart for any fate with both high moral and physical courage.

His extreme courtesy, the courtesy of a gentleman and not the manner of a courtier, impressed every one. His ease of conversation, and public speaking was remarkable, his language simple but strong. His reading was wide, his observation close, and his memory remarkable. After reading a passage once he could repeat it word for word. His knowledge on all subjects was most extensive, yet thorough and complete.

Mr. Davis seldom smiled and was never known to laugh after the fall of the Confederacy.

Mr. Davis was most anxious for a trial in order to vindicate himself and the South in their course, also against the charges made against him: treason, complicity in the assassination of President Lincoln, and responsibility for the suffering at Andersonville and Libby prisons. The United States never brought him to trial, it is said, by the advice of distinguished lawyers. He was released on bond at the end of two years, Cornelius Vanderbilt with Horace Greeley and Gerritt Smith, two strong Abolitionists, being among the bondsmen.

The steamer that bore the illustrious prisoner from Fortress Monroe to Richmond, where the bond was to be made, was met by an immense throng. There was a perfect sea of heads, windows, and roofs were crowded all the way, and the mounted police had to make way for the carriage. The people stood uncovered before the beloved prisoner. When bail was granted and he was released and went to the Spotswood Hotel, the people poured into the hotel and embraced him, and men and women wept aloud.

After spending some time in Canada and in Europe, Mr. Davis made his home in Memphis as the head of an insurance company. This was not a success, and he finally went to Beauvoir. There he wrote his *Rise and Fall of the Confederate Government*, and dedicated it to the women of the Confederacy, who were always devoted to him and who never criticized him, but always had unbounded faith in him. Their loyalty was a source of pride to him, and a consolation in his darkest hours.

He lost his property, and lost one by one his nearest and dearest. His son Jefferson, whom he hoped would be the stay and support of his old age, fell a victim of the yellow scourge in Memphis in 1878. The youngest born, Winnie, survived her father only a few years, and Mrs. Davis, who wrote the valuable *Memoirs* of her illustrious husband, passed into eternal life October, 1906. Only one of the family is left, the eldest daughter, Mrs. Margaret Davis Hayes, of Colorado.

Death came to him in New Orleans, December 5, 1889. As for five days he lay in state in his Confederate gray, guarded by Confederate veterans, many thousands took their last sorrowful look at the beloved dead. Jefferson Davis was a true type of the South in honor, character, and history, and his funeral was the spontaneous outpouring of the love of the South for their leader. Floral offerings were there from all parts of the country. The Bishops of Louisiana and of Mississippi and ministers of all denominations paid tribute to him. The guard of honor for his bier was the Washington Artillery, veterans of the West and of Northern Virginia were the military escort, and the Governors of nine States bore him to his rest. Memorial services were held in every city, town, and hamlet in the South; in churches, schools and legislative halls loving tributes were paid him who so long as life lasted made the cause of the South his cause.

His final resting place is Hollywood Cemetery at Richmond, and on June 3, 1907, the Daughters of the Confederacy with all the pomp and pageantry at their command, unveiled with loving tributes and inspiring speeches a beautiful and handsome monument to him. It is a memorial from the whole South and records the verdict of the South, that Jefferson Davis "was true to his people, his conscience, and his God."

Mrs. Alexander B. White

General Robert E. Lee

The name and character of Robert E. Lee are respected and loved throughout the civilized world. Men of all parties and opinions unite in this sentiment, not only those who thought and fought with him, but those who most violently opposed him.

He was born January 19, 1807. He was the son of Colonel Henry Lee and Annie Hill Carter Lee. His father was called "Lighthorse Harry" on account of his brave service in the Revolutionary War. On one occasion he had surprised and captured the British troops. For this, which was considered one of the most daring deeds of the Revolution, Congress voted him a gold medal.

It was he who said of Washington that he was "first in war, first in peace, and first in the hearts of his countrymen."

As strange as it may seem, it is a fact that Robert E. Lee was born more than a year after his mother had been buried. It happened in this way: General Lee's mother was by no means a strong woman and the physician at Stratford, Virginia, the home of Colonel Henry Lee, was kept in almost constant attendance. Mrs. Lee at times would go into a trance and once during a long attack she was pronounced dead. The body was prepared for burial, and the third day after her supposed death the remains were laid to rest in the family vault in the graveyard of that pretty little Virginia village.

While the sexton was cleaning up and arranging some fresh flowers to be placed on the casket, he heard a faint voice as though of someone calling for help. Of course the old man was very much alarmed, but as he had worked for many years in the "city of the dead" he did not run. He listened closely and the voice was heard again. He was satisfied the voice came from within the casket, so he at once set to work to open it and found that Mrs. Lee was alive. He called for help and soon she was safe in bed at her own home.

Mrs. Lee's recovery was slow, but she regained good health, and more than a year after she was buried alive her youngest son Robert was born and thus came into the world one of the bravest and best loved men of the South.

Robert was only eleven years old when his father died, but he early developed the noble traits of character which made him the great man he was.

When he was but a boy his mother again became an invalid. He was always so bright, cheerful and manly as a boy that he was a source of great comfort to his sick mother. When he left home to attend school his mother said, "How can I do without Robert? He is both son and daughter to me."

Young Lee was very fond of sports of all kinds. He was very fond of swimming in the Potomac. While this was true, he rarely ever left his invalid mother to engage in these sports. He would leave the other boys at play and hurry home every day from school to take his mother out driving. With gentle, loving hands he would assist her to the carriage, and then sitting by her side, care for and entertain her. "You must be cheerful," he would say, or "the drive will not do you any good."

In his home, in the schoolroom, and on the playground he was always faithful and diligent. Whatever is worth doing at all, he thought, is worth doing well.

Of the early life of Lee we know but little. His father just before his death in speaking to a friend, said, "Robert was always good."

He never in his life used any profane language or was guilty of immorality.

Young Lee is described by those who saw him in his youth as a young man of great personal beauty. He was tall and possessed a most perfect figure. He was so graceful in motion that walking seemed to be no exertion to him. His features were handsome and his expression commanding, yet kind and winning. In his manner he was quiet and modest, but self-possessed.

His boyhood life was passed in that part of Virginia which was part of the time amid scenes of war in 1814. While the second war with England was in progress, British ships were robbing Virginia coast cities. He was at that time seven years old and the scenes of war left a lasting impression on his young mind.

His father had been a famous soldier and he, too, wished to enter the army. So at the age of eighteen, he entered the military academy at West Point.

He was a model student, as is proven by the fact that during his entire course of four years he never received a demerit for misconduct. This was an unusual thing in that school. He was very fond of his teacher at West Point and often spoke in highest terms of him. When he graduated there were forty-six in his class and he ranked second of the number.

After he graduated he was put on the Engineer Corps and sent to Florida to build forts.

It was several years after he left West Point before he had much fighting to do. At last in 1846 the war with Mexico and our country broke out. He was made Chief Engineer of the army under General Scott. This was a very responsible position and was filled by him with marked ability. The success of the battle depends largely upon the Engineer, as it is his duty to survey the field, plan the battle and plant the batteries where they will be the most effective.

General Scott was heard more than once to say that his success in Mexico was largely due to the skill, bravery and energy of Robert E. Lee. He declared to General Preston that young Lee was the greatest soldier in America, and long before the breaking out of the Civil War, Scott said, "If the President of the United States should ask my judgment as to the ability of a commander I would say with my dying breath, let it be Robert Lee."

After the Mexican War, he was appointed Superintendent of the Military Academy at West Point. While occupying this position, he introduced a number of changes and reforms which showed his ability as a manager of young men.

A Hero's Choice

Conditions were rapidly developing that would lead to an entire change in the career of this young man. The clouds of the Civil War were gathering, and the critical time came when the States began to secede from the Union.

Lee was Captain in the army of the United States. He loved the Union and it was a sad day for him when his native State seceded. He found himself compelled to choose between the Union and his beloved Virginia. He was offered the command of the armies of the Union. Every influence was brought to bear upon him not to leave the Union army. It was the hardest problem he had ever had to solve. However after consideration he resigned his command in the United States army and went to live or die with Virginia. Such a test proved the true worth of the man.

Someone who saw him on his way to Richmond to join the Confederate forces said he was the handsomest and at the same time the saddest-looking man he ever saw.

The entire South was anxiously awaiting his decision and when it was made in her favor there was universal rejoicing. He took command of the Virginia forces and was afterwards made Commander-in-Chief of the Confederate army.

As General in the Civil War

As General in the Civil War he ranks among the foremost military leaders of all times. Through four years of one of the bloodiest wars known to history, the Confederate army, composed of the flower of Southern manhood, under its matchless leader made a record of victories never surpassed in any warfare — a record of which the South should be very proud.

In a little while after Lee took command, he with a much smaller army attacked the forces of a man by the name of McClellan. This man's army was in its entrenchments and had everything needed for fighting. For seven days the bloody fight continued. At last Lee's army was victorious. Because he was defeated by Lee, McClellan was removed from his position and a man by the name of Pope took his place. But it was not long until Lee defeated him also, and he was removed and McClellan was given his place again. He did not keep his place long, for because he was not at another time able to defeat Lee he was removed and a man by the name of Burnside was made commander. Lee completely defeated the army of Burnside and he was removed and General Hooker was placed in command.

Now General Hooker was very anxious to capture Richmond, which was the Capital of the Confederacy. He said that the Confederate army must "either ingloriously fly or come out from behind its entrenchments, where certain destruction awaited it." A few days after he said this, his army nearly was attacked at the same time in front and rear by Lee and Jackson and it fled in the greatest disorder from the field. General Lee now decided that he would go into the Northern States, so he went into Pennsylvania. At Gettysburg he attacked the Union forces that were in their entrenchments with nearly twice as many men as he had. For three days a most bloody battle was fought. He saw he could not get them out of their entrenchments and of course he could not whip them unless he could get them out. He thought he would try another plan, so he drew his men in line of battle right in front of the enemy, by so doing inviting an attack. He waited for twenty-four hours but they did not attack him, so he went back into Virginia.

For his failure in this attempt he took all the blame on himself and asked President Davis to receive his resignation. He would not accept it. General Lee never boasted. He never spoke ill of the enemy. He prayed for them.

For the first three years of the war the army of Lee in offensive warfare had held every battlefield upon which it had fought except two, and upon these fields, although it failed to defeat the army in entrenchments, it stood on each occasion for twenty-four hours inviting the enemy to attack.

Lee was now to show that in defensive fighting he was a greater master of the art of war than in offensive. Grant with the largest army ever marshaled upon this continent under a single commander, with unlimited resources of men and money, with the world to draw upon for all that was most useful in destructive warfare, advanced upon the army of Lee, wanting in everything but valor, and so many of them were killed that Grant himself said, "it had robbed the cradle and the grave" to fill the gaps between the veterans that still survived. Within about a month there was fought by these two great Generals a series of battles so terrible in their results that their history might well be written in blood. It is said that during this time Grant lost 55,000 men, a number nearly equal to Lee's army at the commencement of the month. In one battle he lost 10,000 men in twenty minutes. That Grant was out-generaled by Lee is shown by his movements. He had started direct to Richmond. Lee's army was in front of him, which army he announced at the beginning of the campaign was his objective.

He did not go to Richmond but turned and crossed the James River, intending to capture Petersburg by surprise. But Lee was there in time and held Grant at bay for ten months. This siege of Petersburg for the Confederates was indeed a time of starvation, exposure, and misery. The army of Lee true to its colors, was literally starving to death. Beef sold for six dollars a pound, and flour at one thousand dollars a barrel. Lee said in pleading with his government for food, that for three days his men had been in line of battle and had not tasted meat. During these days he shared all the hardships with his soldiers. During the whole war he never slept in a house, but with his men in the field. He would not provide his table with abundance when his men were hungry. When his friends sent him food he gave it to his wounded soldiers or sick prisoners.

In an effort to capture Petersburg, Grant burrowed beneath the defences and exploded a gigantic mine. A detachment of Union troops rushed into the "crater" to force their way into the city. The commander did not act promptly and the troops were caught in a death-trap. Lee's guns opened upon the struggling mass of men and about 4,000 were killed or taken prisoners. Grant said this attempt of his was a stupendous failure.

At last after nine months of persistent effort, Grant, with one hundred and thirteen thousand men, well fed, clad, and armed, broke through the lines defended by Lee's forces of forty-nine thousand half-starved, ragged, and shoeless men

Then came the end at Appomattox. General Lee sent to General Gordon to find out the probable result of an attack on the enemy in his direction, and he received the reply, that his corps was worn to a frazzle, and he did not think they could do anything more. After a moment's silence, General Lee said with much feeling, "There is nothing left but to go to General Grant, and I would rather die a thousand deaths."

When the surrender had about been determined, one of the staff officers said, "What will history say of our surrender if there is any possibility of escape? The world will not understand it." To these words General Lee responded, "Yes, yes, it will not understand our situation, but that is not the question. The question is whether it is right; and if it is right I take the responsibility." His deep voice filled with sadness as he said to his staff, "How easily I could get rid of this burden and be at rest. I have only to ride out in view of the enemy and all would be over. But it is our duty to live. What will become of the women and children of the South if we are not here to protect them?"

On that fatal morning of the surrender, he said to one of his staff that he was sorry he had not fallen in one of the last battles. Yet through it all he held wonderful control of himself.

When the two great commanders met in the little brick house at Appomattox to agree on the terms of peace, they presented quite a contrast. One not acquainted with the circumstances would have selected Lee for the conqueror and Grant for the defeated hero. General Lee through respect for the Federal Chieftain was dressed in his best uniform; General Grant was dressed in his mud-bespattered uniform and cavalry boots, for he had come direct from his lines among his soldiers to the place of conference. His plain blue overcoat concealed all signs of rank. It is thought by some that his consideration for General Lee prompted him to avoid all signs of show. When after his meeting with General Grant, General Lee again appeared, a shout of welcome went up from the army. But when they remembered the sad occasion that brought him before them, they at once became silent; every hat was raised and the brown faces of thousands of brave warriors were bathed in tears. As he rode slowly along the lines, hundreds of devoted veterans pressed around their beloved chief trying to take his hand, touch his person, or even lay their hands upon his horse. Then the General with bared head and cheeks bathed with tears bade adieu to the army.

In a few words he said, "Men, we have fought through the war together; I have done my best for you; my heart is too full to say more." He bade them good-bye and told them to return to their homes and become good citizens. He prayed that a merciful God would extend to them His blessing and protection.

Thus ended the military career of one of the greatest captains of history.

General Lee as a Private Citizen

In a few days after the surrender General Lee started for Richmond, riding Traveler, who had carried him so faithfully through the war. He now became a private citizen for the first time in his life. All of General Lee's property had been destroyed by the war and he was absolutely without means.

Yet he refused houses, lands, and money offered him. He was offered large sums of money by business corporations if he would only let them use his name as their president; but he refused them all and accepted the presidency of Washington College at Lexington, Virginia at a small salary, where, as he expressed it, he "could teach young men to do their duty in life."

An English nobleman desired him to accept a mansion and an estate in keeping with his merits and the greatness of an historic family.

He replied, "I am deeply grateful; I cannot desert

my native State in her hour of trouble. I must abide her fortunes, and share her fate."

He was spared to be President of Washington College only five years, but even that brief time proved him to be one of the greatest college presidents this country has ever produced.

He took pains to become acquainted with each student personally, to be really his guide and friend. His success pleased him and his failure pained and grieved him. He worked very hard to make all his students good useful men. One who was a student at Washington College while General Lee was President says the morning he entered college he went to the office of General Lee to get instructions as to his work. He entered with awe, expecting to see the great warrior as he had pictured him in his own imagination. General Lee was alone, looking over a paper. He arose and received him with a quiet, gentlemanly dignity that was so natural and easy and kind that the feeling of awe was left at the door. He was so different from the great warrior his imagination had pictured, he was so gentle, kind, and almost motherly, in his bearing that he thought there must be some mistake about it.

General Lee had the same treatment for the poor as he had for the rich. He treated a student with the same courtesy that he would the most noted man in the world. When asked by a student for a copy of his rules, General Lee said, "Young man, we have no printed rules. We have but one rule here, and it is that every student must be a gentleman."

It is said that General Lee rarely spoke to any one; occasionally he would say something to one of the boys as he passed, but never more than a word. He seemed to avoid contact with men and to be bowed down with a broken heart. The expression on his face seemed to show that he bore the grief of a whole nation.

General Lee was always a very modest man. Although General, he would never wear the sign of his rank. He wore only three stars on his collar, the insignia of a Colonel. He was asked one day why he did not wear the full sign of his rank and not that of a Colonel.

The modest chieftain replied, "Oh, I don't care for display. And the truth is that the rank of Colonel is about as high as I ought ever to have gotten."

A few days after he went to Lexington to live he rode up Main Street on his old war horse Traveler, and as he passed up the street the citizens cheered him. He at once went to his home and never again appeared on the streets on horseback. He always took his afternoon rides, but ever afterward he rode out back of the college campus.

General Lee was a most fair-minded man and was entirely free from bitterness of feeling. A lady who had lost her husband in the war and brought her two sons to his college, indulged in expressions of great bitterness toward the North. To her he said gently, "Madam, do not train up your children in hostility to the government of the United States. Remember that we are one country now. Bring up your boys to be Americans."

Another incident showing his freedom from bitterness is told by a citizen of the North. He says, "One day I saw General Lee standing at his gate talking pleasantly to an humbly clad man who seemed very much pleased at the courtesy of the great chieftain. He passed on as I came up. General Lee said to me pointing to the retreating form, 'That is one of our old soldiers who is in needy circumstances.' I took it for granted that he was some veteran

Confederate, when the noble chieftain added, 'He fought
on the other side, but we must not think of that.' I found
out afterwards that he had not only spoken kindly to the
old soldier 'who fought on the other side,' but had made
a liberal contribution to his necessities."

His forgiving spirit is shown on another occasion.
Soon after the surrender when most people's hearts were
filled with bitterness, a gentleman was requested by the
Federal Commander to inform General Lee that he was
about to be indicted in the United States Court for treason. In delivering this information the gentleman expressed
his violent indignation at such proceeding. General Lee did
not seem to share these feelings. The threat of being indicted as a traitor had no other effect upon him than to
bring a smile to his lips, and taking the hand of his friend
as he rose to go he said in his mildest tones, "We must
forgive our enemies. I can truly say that not a day has
passed since the war began that I have not prayed for
them."

It is hard to believe that there is any one who for
a moment thinks that General Lee was a traitor. If he was
a traitor, so was George Washington. Their cases are very
similar. Washington was a Virginian like Lee and was also
a British subject; he had fought under the British flag as
Lee had fought under the flag of the United States. When
in 1776 Virginia seceded from the British empire, he went
with his State just as Lee went eighty-five years later.
Washington became a noted General in the army, known
by those who opposed it as "rebels," just as Lee later was
a noted General in an army known as "rebels." Only in the
outcome were their cases different. Then if one was a traitor so was the other.

Two ladies in Baltimore were heard to say one day

"Everybody and everything — his family, his friends, his horse, and his dog — loves General Lee." The secret of this was he loved them. He was very fond of animals. In his letters to his family he frequently asked about the pets.

One stormy night his little girl's cat was heard crying under his window. He got out of bed, opened the window and called pussy to come in. The window was so high that she could not jump up to it. He then took one of his wife's crutches and held it so far out of the window that he became wet from the falling rain, but he persuaded the cat to climb up the crutch and into the window before he thought of dry clothes for himself.

His devotion to his family was beautiful. This noble man who with the responsibility of a large army upon him and while planning his battle would take time to write his wife and children letters filled with affection and loving advice.

His son says, "He was the most punctual man I ever saw. He was always ready for family prayers, for meals and met every engagement, social and business, at the moment. He expected all of us to be the same, and taught us the use and necessity of forming such habits for the convenience of others. I never saw him late at church. He used to appear some minutes before the rest of us and joke my mother for being late, and for forgetting something at the last moment. When he could no longer wait on her, he would say that he is off and would go on to church by himself or with some of the children who were ready."

General Lee was never idle, and what he had to do he performed with care and precision.

Last Days

During the trying campaign of 1863 General Lee contracted a severe sore throat. Some years later he was attacked with heart disease, and was troubled with weariness and depression.

In March, 1870, General Lee, at the wishes of friends and physicians, made a six-weeks' visit to Georgia and Florida. He returned much benefitted. But as he said to his son, he was never to be well again.

In September, 1870, he entered upon his duties in the college as usual. On Wednesday, September 28th, in the forenoon, he performed all the duties of his office, and after dinner at four o'clock attended a vestry meeting of his church. The afternoon was chilly and wet and a rain set in, which did not stop until it resulted in a great flood, the most memorable and destructive in that region for a hundred years.

The meeting lasted until after seven o'clock. They were discussing the rebuilding of the church and the increase of the minister's salary. The amount required for the salary lacked a sum much greater than General Lee's proportion of the subscription, yet he said in a low tone, "I will give that sum."

When he returned home he found his family waiting supper for him. He took his place at the table standing to say grace. The effort was in vain; his lips could not utter the prayer of the heart. When he saw he could not speak, he quietly took his seat. He seemed to realize that the hour had come when all the cares and anxieties of his busy life were at an end. He was soon placed on the bed from which he was never to rise again. When his son made some remark as to his getting well he shook his head and pointed upward. He gradually grew worse and soon after nine o'clock on the morning of October 12th, he closed his eyes and his soul passed peacefully from earth.

When the wires flashed the sad news that General Lee was dead, grief filled every heart. The tolling of bells, flags at half-mast, and public meetings of citizens wearing mourning, showed in every portion of the Southland the great love for the dead hero.

It is said that in at least ten thousand Southern homes tears came to the eyes of not only women but of strong men.

"His funeral services were very simple. There was no sermon or remarks. One of the hymns sung was his favorite, 'How Firm a Foundation.' And they laid away in the vault all that was mortal of Robert Edward Lee. What they laid away was little; what remained on the outside of the tomb was much — the memory of the life and character of the greatest Virginian, the greatest Southerner, the greatest American."

General Lee's Faithful Horse, Traveler

One day a soldier stopped at a farm in Greenbrier county, West Virginia, to purchase a horse for his brother, a Major in the Confederate army. He was shown the best horses from the stables and meadows. Finally after all had been carefully examined a large gray was selected. Some gold was counted out by the soldier and a bridle and saddle were put on the horse.

As he was ridden away that day, little did he think that he was leaving all the treasures of peace behind him. For four years he had passed a quiet untroubled life in green meadow and warm stable. But now he was off to war.

It was not long until he found himself in the midst of a camp. He was surrounded by soldiers, all of whom were admiring his fine parts and easy gait. Every one had a word of praise for him. He must have been a fine horse, for General Lee said he had a fine form: deep chest, short back, flat legs, small head, broad forehead, small ears, quick eyes, small feet, and black mane and tail.

One day General Lee arrived in camp. He was a fine judge of a horse, and was very much attracted by the beauty of the "gray colt," as he called him. He said to his owner, "Major, I shall need that horse before the war is over."

In a short time General Lee left camp to take command in South Carolina. Some months later the Third Regiment was ordered to that State. In this regiment was the "gray colt." It was not long until General Lee chanced to see him. He again expressed his great admiration for the horse, whereupon the Major offered to give the horse to him. General Lee would not accept him on those terms, but said he would like to buy him. So he was bought and was renamed "Traveler."

How proud this gray colt would have been could he have understood that he was to have the honor of carrying the "most noted and honored man of the Confederate army — the best loved man of the South."

When the army returned to Virginia it was on the back of Traveler that General Lee rode. On this long journey many horses failed and sank by the wayside, but Traveler was never known to tire.

On one occasion General Lee reviewed his army and rode Traveler. The army was in divisions, and it was necessary, in order to make the review, to ride around every division. General Lee set forth in company with his

staff, some of whom were on very fine horses. Traveler set
the pace at a steady lope. The distance to be traveled was
fifteen miles. One by one the other horses gave out and
new ones took their places. Traveler went the whole
course and showed no signs of being tired. Not a horse
that started with him was able to go the distance at his
gait.

Among the soldiers the horse was as well-known
as was his master. Wherever the gray horse went bearing
General Lee a shout went up. The horse and master were
never separated. General Lee said, "He carried me through
the Seven Days' battle around Richmond, the second
Manassas, and Sharpsburg, Fredericksburgh, the last day
at Chancellorsville to Pennsylvania, at Gettysburgh, and
back again. From the commencement of the campaign in
1864 at Orange until its close around Petersburgh, the
saddle was seldom off his back."

From this time on the fortunes of the war began to
change. The master whom he had carried through many
victories he bore now through much defeat. The men who
cheered now as he passed by had faces showing hunger
and suffering. The stricken South could hold her own but
little longer. One day the last stand was taken, the last
battle was fought. The cause which had led so many must
be given up.

From Appomattox Traveler carried his master,
now a prisoner of war, to Richmond. It is said, that as the
well-known horse and rider came unheralded through the
streets, Southern citizens and Northern soldiers recogniz-
ing them raised their hats in silent respect or emotion as
the two passed by. At East Franklin Street where General
Lee dismounted and made his way to his waiting family,
crowds gathered around the gray horse who had carried

his master so long and so well and some put their arms around his neck and with tears kissed him.

After the war was ended and General Lee had retired to private life, Traveler was still his master's loved friend and companion. There was nothing General Lee enjoyed more than a good long ride on Traveler. His affection for his horse was very deep, and strong. In a letter written from the Springs one summer he said, "How is Traveler? Tell him I miss him dreadfully, and have repented of our separation but once — and that is the whole time since we parted." As a proof of this bond between them Mrs. S. P. Lee tells a very pretty story: One afternoon the General rode down to the canal-boat landing. He dismounted, tied Traveler to a post. Soon someone called out that Traveler was loose. Sure enough, the gallant gray was making his way up the road, increasing his speed as a number of boys and men tried to catch him. The General at once stepped out, called the crowd to stand still, and advancing a few steps gave a peculiar low whistle. At the first sound, Traveler stopped and pricked up his ears. The General whistled a second time, and the horse with a glad whinny, turned and trotted quietly back to his master.

Time passed pleasantly on until the autumn of 1870 when his tender master lay sick upon his deathbed. Many times during his last days did the master inquire after his faithful horse and companion. Doubtless Traveler longingly waited for the kind hand and gentle voice of the master, but he waited in vain, for he had gone to that home where there are neither wars nor strifes, but one eternal peace.

After the death of the General, Traveler was petted more than ever. He was permitted to go where he pleased about the place.

But he did not long survive his master. In June after General Lee's death it was noticed one day that he was lame. On examination a small nail was found in his hoof. It was extracted and nothing more thought of the matter. In a few days the hostler reported that Traveler was not well. It was soon found that he was suffering with lockjaw. The two physicians who had attended General Lee in his last illness were now called to attend his famous war horse. His sufferings were great. All that skill could do was done. When he could no longer stand, a mattress was laid on the stable floor for him to lie on. But nothing was of any avail. The good horse soon died, beloved and mourned by all.

Truly has it been said that the qualities which have endeared General Lee to so many — courage, bravery, fidelity, gentleness, and fortitude — these qualities were shared by Traveler, and for these reasons, he too, shall be remembered.

Some time after the death of Traveler, his bones were preserved and packed in a box, and in this manner Mr. E. A. Craighill of Lynchburgh, Virginia found them. He at once started a movement to preserve them in a more permanent form. Mr. Joseph Bryan, a wealthy and large-minded citizen secured permission to have the bones cleaned and mounted as they may be seen today.

The story of Lee and his faithful horse will be remembered and rehearsed by children of future generations as by those of today.

General "Stonewall" Jackson

At Clarksburgh, Virginia, on the 21st of January, 1824, there was born one of the most unique characters of American history. It was Thomas Jonathan Jackson. He was descended from Scotch-Irish stock and inherited many of the qualities of his ancestors. He was left a penniless orphan when three years old and in his manly effort to support himself he soon showed the "stuff of which heroes are made." At six years of age he went to live with his uncle. Here he remained working on the farm and attending school long enough to get an ordinary English education.

An interesting story is told by judge H.C. McWhorter which shows what a high sense of honor he had even at the early age of ten years. The uncle with whom Tom, as he was familiarly known, lived had a mill situated on the banks of the West Fork River. This river was well stocked with fish, among which none was sought after so eagerly as that fine game fish called "pike." Tom partially supplied the demand of the limited fish market at the little village of Weston. One day Tom proposed to Mr. Kester that he would let him have all the pike he caught a foot long or over for fifty cents each. Mr. Kester accepted the proposition and the trade was made.

Tom continued to perform his contract faithfully, and sold Mr. Kester every pike he caught of the "regulation length," until one day he was seen by Col. Talbott going through town, making straight for Kester's, bending under the weight of a pike three feet long.

"Hello, Tom," said Col. Talbott. "That's a fine fish you have. I want to buy it."

Tom, without any seeming interest in what the Colonel was saying and without halting replied, "Sold to Mr. Kester."

"That can't be. You have not seen Mr. Kester. I will give you a dollar for it."

"I tell you it is sold, and it is not mine to sell."

"What is Mr. Kester to give you for it?"

"Fifty cents."

"I'll give you a dollar and a quarter for it."

Tom with an indignant look said, "If you get any of this pike, you will have to get it from Mr. Kester."

On presenting the fish to Mr. Kester, that gentleman said, "Tom, this is a splendid pike. I think I shall have to give you a dollar for it; fifty cents is not enough."

Tom replied, "No, sir; that is your pike at fifty cents, and I will not take more for it. Besides you have bought a good many from me that were pretty short." Thus the transaction closed.

At the age of sixteen he was so well thought of that the justices of the County Court of Lewis county elected him Constable. While Constable he learned of a vacancy from his Congressional District in the Military Academy at West Point. He determined to make a journey to Washington and seek the appointment. So he set out at once and traveled the distance on foot. He in his suit of homespun, and with his leathern saddlebags over his shoulders appeared before the Member of Congress from his district. The Congressman presented him to the Secretary of War, who was so much pleased with the youth's determination that he at once made out his appointment to West Point.

The personal appearance of Jackson when he entered West Point was such as to attract attention. He was clad in gray homespun, a wagoner's hat, and large, heavy brogan shoes. Weather-stained saddlebags were over his shoulders. He had an awkward step, cold, bright gray eyes and thin, firm lips.

He was poorly prepared to enter the Academy and barely "squeezed through" on the entrance examination. At first he hung about the foot of his class. At the first January examination all below him failed and were sent home. He was foot and probably would have been cut off also, but his teachers saw in him such a determined intention to succeed that they felt sure he would improve; and he did.

At a certain hour at night taps were sounded and then all lights had to be put out. A few minutes before this time, "Old Jack," as he was called, would fill his fireplace with wood, so as to have a bright, glowing fire when lights had to be put out. Then he would lie down on the floor and study his lessons by the light. It was not long till he began to rise in his class.

After four years of hard study he was graduated number seventeen in a class of sixty. One who knew him intimately well expressed the confident belief that if the course had been a little longer he would have graduated at the head of his class.

At the time of his graduation the United States was at war with Mexico, and the young graduate was assigned to duty under General Taylor. It was some months before his regiment had an opportunity for active service. For his splendid behavior he was soon promoted to the rank of Captain.

From the moment Jackson entered upon his duties in the army he showed that intense earnestness which was the characteristic of all his conduct.

He was a strict disciplinarian. He obeyed every order to the letter and expected all under him to do the same.

An officer once galloped up to him in the midst of a battle and said, "General Jackson, did you order me to charge that battery," pointing to it.

"Yes, sir, I did. Have you obeyed the order?"

"Why, no. General, I thought there must be some mistake. My men would be cut to pieces in a moment if we should move across that field."

"Sir," said Jackson, his eyes flashing fire and his voice and manner showing excitement, and even rage, "I always try to take care of my wounded and bury my dead. Obey that order, Sir, and do it at once."

One day he called a certain Colonel to him and said: "I thought Colonel that the orders were for you to move in the rear instead of the front of General ——."

"Yes, I know that, General Jackson; but my men were ready to start before his and I thought it would be bad to keep them waiting and that it really made no difference anyhow."

"I want you to understand, Sir," was the almost fierce reply, "that you must obey my orders first and reason about them afterwards. Consider yourself under arrest, Sir, and march to the rear of your brigade."

The following incident will show how strictly he

obeyed orders. When John Brown made an attempt to arouse an insurrection in Virginia, the Governor ordered the State troops and the corps of Cadets to be held ready for immediate service. General Smith, superintendent of the corps, promptly obeyed the orders. Major Jackson reported at the guard-room ready for the field. General Smith, after attending to some matters, said, "Major Jackson, you will remain as you are until further orders."

At that time Jackson was seated upon a camp-stool in the guard-room with his saber across his knees. The next morning General Smith went to the guard-room and found Jackson sitting on the camp-stool with his saber across his knees. He exclaimed, "Why, Major, why are you here?"

"Because you ordered me to remain here as I was last night, and I have done so."

After the war with Mexico had come to an end, Jackson was stationed for two years at Fort Hamilton, and was then ordered to Fort Meade, Florida. He remained but a short time, as the climate was so injurious to his health that he was compelled to return.

*   *   *   *

In the year 1851, he was elected Professor of Natural Philosophy at the Virginia Military Institute.

Many times it is the case that truly great men have to pass through a period when their worth is not known and often they are the subjects of ridicule. Such was the painful experience of Jackson at the Virginia Institute. He made little reputation as a professor, for while thoroughly acquainted with his subject, he lacked that "aptness to teach" so essential to a successful teacher, and the Cadets were always playing pranks on him.

Jackson feared no man. While a professor in the Virginia Institute, he arrested and caused a distinguished Cadet to be expelled for breaking some of the regulations. The Cadet was a scholar and soldier. He had worked hard for years and now found himself deprived of his diploma which was the object of his long endeavor. He was very angry at such harshness and vowed he would horse-whip Jackson, and prepared himself to carry out his threat. He was a powerful and daring young man and was able to do Jackson great bodily harm. The friends of both were very anxious. Jackson was urged to have the young man bound over to keep the peace. This would require him to swear that he was in bodily fear of his enemy. He said, "I will not do it, for it would be false. I do not fear him; I fear no man."

When the war between the States came on he had this young fellow made Brigadier, and he became one of the most distinguished Generals of the war.

Jackson was noted for the quickness with which he decided what to do.

One day his quick decision prevented what might have been a bloody collision.

The students of the Military Institute at Lexington, Virginia were in the habit of engaging in heated discussions with the natives on the subject of secession. Sometimes these discussions would end in blows and in the majority of cases the students found themselves no match for the rugged mountaineers. So frequently did they get the worst of the encounters that at last they resolved to resort to arms.

One day it was reported to General Smith, who was in charge of the Institute, that the boys were getting their guns from the armory and that they were going down town to do battle with the citizens. General Smith seemed completely upset and did not know anything to do to prevent what promised to be a bloody collision.

While Jackson was at dinner, word of the movement of the students reached him. He at once left the table and went to the front of the house. Sure enough here came the students pell-mell down the road, some hatless, all with guns and in great excitement. Jackson stepped to a horse block in front of the house, and just as the head of the column was passing, called out in most commanding tones, "Halt! Front face!" The boys halted instantly. "Well, young men," he asked in his mildest tone, "where are you going?" One of the foremost told in few words their troubles and their intention to right them. "Well," he said, "that's very well, perhaps, but who is your leader?"

They acknowledged that they had none. "Do you not think it a little unwise to go out on an enterprise such as this without a leader?" They said that it seemed so.

"How would you like me for your leader?" Nothing could please them better.

"Well, then, I think as we are going on a serious enterprise we had better try to organize. Suppose we get out here in the road and drill a little." This was done. He got them over in a field and drilled them until they were pretty well tired out. Then he brought them back into the road and from the horse block he made them a little speech on the foolishness of such actions which they had planned, saying that some of them might get killed, to the grief of their friends at home, or some of the townspeople might be slain. "Now be good boys and go back to your studies." They all went back to their work. In this we see the real Jackson, ready and alert.

It was not long until he went off to the great war

between the States and won fame at once.

He marched with his Cadets to Camp Lee, at Richmond, where he began drilling new troops that were constantly flocking to the camp. His was known as the "Stonewall Brigade," and was one of the most famous of the Civil War. It was composed to a large extent of very young men, many of them but fifteen years of age. Very few had ever experienced hardships of any kind. They had come from homes of luxury to enter upon a life which required their most heroic efforts.

The battle of Manassas, the first great battle of the war, will always occupy a place among the great conflicts of the world. The fortunes of this memorable day were decided by the First Brigade, whose gallant commander here first received the proud title of "Stonewall."

At Bull Run, the two opposing armies met, the Federals with 55,000 men and the Confederates with 31,500. The fighting began early in the morning by a furious attack on the Confederate left. The Southerners fought hard but were being pressed back by the Federals. For a time this onward rush was checked by General Bee. Finally he had to give way and his men began to run. He tried to recall his men but he could not. His voice could not be heard. At the moment when he was about to give up in despair a courier dashed up to tell him that help was coming. He rushed out to meet the rescuers and in a moment was face to face with Jackson. "General," he cried, "they are beating us back." The stern face of Jackson showed no signs of fear as he replied, "Sir, we will give them the bayonet." General Bee's men came rushing on with the Federals in hot pursuit but Jackson's men stood firm. The very sight was inspiring. Bee plunged in among his men and shouted, "Look, there is Jackson standing like a stone wall. Let us determine to die here and we will conquer." In an instant the fortunes of the day had changed. During the day, Jackson's Brigade made many a gallant charge. The result was the Confederates won the day.

The following day in a letter to his wife, Jackson wrote, "Whilst great credit is due to other parts of our great army, God made my brigade more instrumental than any other in repulsing the main attack."

In this great battle he was wounded in the hand but refused to leave the field. While the surgeons were dressing his wounds, President Davis rode on the field, and Jackson pushing aside the surgeons tossed his cadet cap in the air and exclaimed, "Hurrah for the President. Give me ten thousand men and I will be in Washington tonight."

For three days after the battle of Manassas he waited and hoped for the order which would tell him to advance on Washington. Had it come the result of the Civil War might have been different.

In a few months he was sent on the famous "Valley Campaign." His campaign is now studied in military academies in Europe because of its able strategy, rapid movements, and heroic fighting. In thirty-two days, Jackson and his "foot cavalry" had marched 400 miles, defeated three armies, two of which were completely routed, captured twenty pieces of artillery, 4,000 prisoners and immense quantities of stores of all kinds. He did this with a loss of fewer than 1,000 men killed, wounded and missing, and with a force of only 15,000 men, while there were at least 60,000 men opposed to him.

*   *   *   *

Jackson's successful career in the Civil War was not a long one. It was only for two years; yet he crowded into those two years more successful work than any other soldier on either side.

His success was due to his bravery, skill, and attention to minute details. He had an interview with his quartermaster, his commissary, and his medical officer every day, and he was at all times familiar with the condition of these departments.

He was not content with simply learning what his maps could teach him of the country through which he expected to move. He would have frequent interviews with the citizens of the place, and would personally view out the ground on which he expected to fight. Often at night, when the army was wrapped in sleep, he would ride out alone to inspect roads by which on the morrow he expected to move to strike the enemy.

But the end of his career was fast approaching. On May 2nd, 1863, Jackson suddenly fell upon the Federal forces near Chancellorsville and drove them before him in great confusion. Darkness came on and the lines of the various divisions became mixed and disordered. While trying to reform his lines for further pursuit there came a sudden lull in the fighting. At this time Jackson rode forward to view out the situation.

Captain W. F. Randolph, who was with Jackson, says:

> We advanced down the turnpike a short distance toward the enemy. As we proceeded we heard a few random shots in the woods to our right. Our men on our left, excited by these shots, commenced firing across the road into the woods, not in regular volleys, but just here and there along the line. General Jackson turned to me and said, "Order those men to stop that fire and tell the officers not to permit another shot without orders." I rode up

and down the line and gave the order to both men and officers, telling them they were endangering the lives of General Jackson and his escort. But in vain; those in front would cease as I gave the order, but the firing would break out above or below me.

I rode back to General Jackson and said, "General, it is impossible to stop them. We had better pass through their lines and get in the woods behind them."

"Very well said," was the reply. So turning, our little company started to pass through their line and get beyond the range of their fire.

A few more seconds would have placed us in safety, for we were not over three yards from the line; but as I looked up I saw the long line of bayonets rise and all point toward us. I knew what was coming, and driving spurs into the flanks of my horse, a powerful animal and full of spirit, he rose high in the air and as we passed over the line, the thunder crash from hundreds of rifles burst full in our faces. I looked back as my horse made the leap and everything had gone down like leaves before a storm. The only living being besides myself that passed through that stream of fire was a horse. My horse was shot in several places, my clothing and saddle were filled with bullet holes, yet I escaped without a wound, the only living man to tell the fearful story of that inexcusable and unwarranted fire.

As soon as possible, I rushed back to the road and there I saw the saddest tragedy of the war revealed in the fullest horror. I saw the General's horse, which I recognized at once, standing by the road with his head bent low and a stream of blood flowing from his neck. This was the faithful horse Jackson had ridden for a long time — the horse that was said not to know how to run except toward the enemy. I rushed to the spot and found the General himself lying in the edge of the woods. He seemed to be dead. I raised his head and shoulders on my arm. He groaned heavily.

"Are you much hurt General?" I asked as soon as I could find voice.

"Wild fire that, Sir; wild fire," he replied in his usual rapid way. This was all he said.

Medical aid was hastily summoned, and although the wounds caused him great pain he never complained.

He was placed on a litter and born away by his staff while under heavy fire from the enemy. One of the men carrying him was shot and the litter fell violently to the ground, causing General Jackson much pain. He was taken to the field infirmary and there his arm was amputated.

For the first few days he seemed to be recovering, but it was not long until examination showed that pneumonia had set in.

His wife was sent for. She came and remained until the end came. He passed away peacefully on Sunday, May 10, 1863. He faced death as calmly on his bed of pain as he had on the field of battle.

A few moments before his death he called out in delirium, "Order A.P. Hill to prepare for action. Pass the infantry rapidly to the front. Tell Major Hawks...." Here the sentence was left unfinished. A sweet smile overspread his face, and he murmured quietly, "Let us pass over the river and rest under the shades of the trees," and without pain or struggle his spirit passed away and he had won his last battle.

Character of General Jackson

There probably was no more ambitious man in the Southern Confederacy than General Jackson. He was not ambitious as the world usually regards ambition. He was ambitious in the true and noble sense which is free from the coarse bids for popular favor. He was a man of extreme sensitiveness. When he came under the fitful cloud of President Davis' displeasure, he was so affected by it that he determined to resign his position in the army, but by the persuasion of friends he was induced to withdraw his resignation.

He was a man of feminine tenderness combined with a very strong will.

The following story is told of him illustrating his extreme tenderness to whatever was weak or helpless: He, while staying at the house of a friend one cold wintry night, showed much concern for a little delicate girl of the family, and urged them to see that her bed was comfortable. After the family had retired, he was seen to leave his bed and go to the bedside of the little girl, where he spent some minutes tucking the bed clothes around her and making the little creature as comfortable as possible. The large, rough hand that did this gentle task, was the same that wielded the thunderbolt of battle.

He was a person of almost superhuman endurance. Neither heat nor cold seemed to make the slightest impression on him. He cared nothing for good quarters or dainty fare. He often slept on the ground, wrapped in his blanket. His watchfulness was marvelous; he never seemed to sleep; he let nothing pass without his personal scrutiny.

After all, the crowning glory of Jackson, as it was also of Lee, was his humble, simple-hearted piety, his firm trust in Christ as his personal Savior, his godly walk and conversation, and his life of active effort for the good of others.

He spent much time in prayer and in the study of the Bible. His servant man, a faithful Negro, would sometimes go out early in the morning to the officers' camp and say, "Gentlemen, there's gwine to be hard fighting today; Mars Tom was on his knees praying all night long."

The Captain of his bodyguard tells us, "Just before the battle of Chancellorsville, General Jackson and I stopped in a wood, dismounted and tied our horses. We sat down on a log. Jackson began to examine a map before him, and being very tired, I soon fell asleep. Waking suddenly I turned and saw the General kneeling with his arms resting on the log in earnest prayer. I said, surely this great soldier, who holds such close and constant communion with his Maker, must certainly succeed in whatever he undertakes."

It has been said that so long as "Stonewall" Jackson lived the Union forces could not prevail against his prayers.

Prayer-meetings and "revivals" were common occurrences in his camp and in them he was quite active. Eternity alone will tell how far the great revivals in General Lee's army, through which over 15,000 of his soldiers were brought to Christ, were in answer to the prayers and in blessing upon the labors of this great "Soldier of the Cross," as well as soldier of his country.

This great commander must stand as an example for our youth to follow. His whole success may be summed up in three words: "Devotion to duty."

General Joseph Eggleston Johnston

General Joseph Eggleston Johnston was born in Prince Edward county, Virginia on February 3rd, 1807, and died on March 21st, 1891. He was one of the leading Generals of the Southern Confederacy, and was beloved by his own people as well as by his prominent opponents.

He will always be known as a great General, hero, author, and a Christian gentleman, a devoted friend and a loving husband; he will live in history as an able leader, worthily occupying a place in the front rank of the world's military chiefs.

Johnston's name passes into history with ever growing brightness as his war campaigns are better understood. Colonel Chesney, the eminent English military writer, in an article entitled, "Lee and Johnston," says, "It is not too much to declare that Johnson, doing what he did with the limited means at his command, is a feat that should leave his name in the annals of defensive war."

As he was educated at West Point, it fell to his lot to take masses of undisciplined troops and to make armies out of them, or to be placed in charge of soldiers, demoralized and disorganized by disasters caused by incapacity of others. By the time he had them in order he would be superseded in command for someone else to reap the glory that resulted from carrying out his plans, for he is acknowledged to be the greatest strategist of the entire Civil War.

Johnston was of Scotch descent. The first immigrant of the Virginia Johnstones was Peter, which was the family name of the oldest son as far back as can be traced. He was born in Annam, Scotland in 1710, but emigrated from Edinburgh in 1727, and settled on James River at Osborne's Landing. His business seemed to absorb him entirely, and at last at the age of fifty-two years he decided to marry. He married a widow, Mrs. Martha Rogers, in 1761, a daughter of Mr. John Butler, who lived on the Appomattox, below Petersburg.

After his marriage, he moved to Prince Edward county and settled near Farmville, and called his estate "Cherry's Grove." They were people of refinement. Mr. Johnston gave one hundred acres of land to the founding of Hampden Sidney College, where his three sons were educated, one of whom was the father of General Johnston. His oldest son, Peter, while there at school, hearing the stories and exploits of friends in the Continental army, soon forgot paternal instructions and became an ardent patriot. At the age of seventeen, he ran away from College, and in 1780 enlisted in the legion of Light Horse Harry Lee. He served with him during the remainder of the Revolution. Notwithstanding his age, by the end of the war he had risen to the rank of a Lieutenant and was a favorite of Colonel Lee and his whole legion. Thus the basis of the friendship between the families of Lee and Johnston was laid in the last century, by the fathers of the two great Southern leaders of the war between the States — a friendship that was still closer between the sons.

At the end of the Revolution, Lieutenant Johnston, though only twenty years old, decided to select law as his profession. He soon rose to prominence in law and politics. In 1788, he married a niece of Patrick Henry. To them was born a family of nine sons and one daughter. All his sons rose to prominence in their States, as jurists, statesmen, and writers. The eighth son of this marriage was Joseph Eggleston Johnston, who was born at Cherry Grove, Prince Edward county, Virginia on February 3rd, 1807. He was named for Joseph Eggleston, a military associate of his father, and Captain of the company in Lee's Legion in which his father was Lieutenant.

In 1811 his father was appointed a Judge of the General Court of Virginia and moved to Abington. At that time, that section of the State was thinly settled and conditions of life were extremely hard. The town was in the heart of a forest and the country rugged and mountainous and roads difficult. Young Joe was thus early accustomed to outdoor life, and his extended hunting expeditions and the hours spent in his saddle over rough mountain roads, was a fine training for him to fatigue and hardships and familiarizing him with danger. To this early experience he owed his fine constitution, which he retained through life, notwithstanding his numerous wounds and long continued exposure.

He was taught by both of his parents and attended Abington Academy, where he showed a fondness for classical studies. As a boy he heard thrilling accounts of the battle of Kings Mountain. Such narratives fired the mind of Joseph and as he naturally loved things military, he organized his young friends into a military company and drilled them. As he grew older he still wanted to be a soldier and it seemed to be the natural bent of his mind and not a mere boyish fancy. In 1825, at the age of eighteen, he was admitted as a cadet at West Point, and was a classmate of Robert E. Lee, and they soon became fast friends. He stood very well in his classes and made the most of his opportunities. On account of his eyes he could only study during the day or he might have stood better. In a class of forty-six he graduated thirteenth in 1829. Robert E. Lee was second and Charles Mason of New York stood at the head. From the time of graduation until 1837, he served mainly on garrison duty.

His first experience in real war was in 1832 in the Black Hawk expedition under General Scott, and the next in the expedition against the Florida Indians in 1836. In 1842 he was again sent to fight the Seminoles, and was with General North when they finally conquered the next year.

During the time of rest before the Mexican War he met and married Lydia McLane.

When hostilities with Mexico began, Johnston secured an assignment with General Winfield Scott's army and was in the whole campaign, from Vera Cruz to the surrender of the Capital. When Vera Cruz yielded, Captains Robert E. Lee and Joseph E. Johnston were appointed to make terms of surrender. In the storming of Chapultepec he led his men with much gallantry. He was wounded three times and was breveted Lieutenant-Colonel. General Scott said of him, "Johnston is a great soldier, but he has an unfortunate knack of getting himself shot in nearly every engagement."

At the close of the Mexican War, he was engaged in topographical engineer work in Texas, and on Western River improvements. In the summer of 1860 General Jesup, Quarter-Master General of the United States, died.

As he was next in rank to General Scott, the question of his successor was very important, on account of General Scott's advanced age. When General Scott was asked to name the man he considered the best fitted for the office, he submitted four names, Joseph E. Johnston, Robert E. Lee, Albert Sidney Johnston, and Charles F. Smith. Joseph E. Johnston was selected and his commission dated June 28th, 1860; this made him Brigadier-General. He enjoyed his new honors but a short time. As the war clouds arose, he knew old ties must be broken. He was personally opposed to secession and saw with grief the withdrawal of the Southern States from the Union, but waited for the action of Virginia, to which he felt he owed his first allegiance.

When President Lincoln's call for troops forced Virginia from neutrality and compelled her to choose her side in the coming contest, Johnston considered it his duty to follow his State, and that it was the only honorable course to pursue.

* * * *

Virginia seceded on April 17, 1861. Johnston heard it late on April 19th, resigned next day and two days later his resignation was presented to the Secretary of War, with a request for an order announcing immediate acceptance — a request which was granted, though, as the Secretary stated, with great regret. The next day he and Mrs. Johnston left for Richmond, where he arrived on the 25th and reported to Governor Letcher, who at once made him Major-General in the State service, and on the day following he was appointed to the command of all the State forces about Richmond. Lee had reached Richmond two days earlier, and his commission antedated Johnston's by two days. It was, of course, a great sacrifice for him to give up his position in the United States army. He was the highest officer in that army who resigned and his rank, considered in connection with the extreme age of General Scott, would soon have made him senior officer of the National armies.

The only property he brought with him from Washington, was his father's Revolutionary sword; he said he had promised his father never to draw it except in defense of his native State, and he thought the time had come to use it. After the State of Virginia had entered into Convention with the Southern Confederacy, the Confederate Congress authorized the appointment of five Brigadier-Generals, and Lee and Johnston were two of these appointed. Johnston commanded the force which occupied Harper's Ferry on May, 1861, but he soon saw the place was untenable and that Winchester was the energetic point for every purpose. He held in check the Union forces of more than 30,000 strong under General Robert Patterson, and hurled his own from the mountains upon McDowell, which was the master stroke of Manassas. Johnston's rear column under Kirby Smith, coming upon the field just as Barnard Bee was falling, and Jackson's Stonewall, a last Gibralter, was wavering. It was a victory which almost proved a defeat, and one hard to pursue.

After the battle of Manassas, Johnston again devoted himself to the organization and equipment of the army of Northern Virginia. He was fitted for this work, and time after time during the war, took raw, disorganized or discouraged troops and put them in order.

In the Spring of 1862, Johnston was ordered to watch the four routes by which McClellen might advance to Richmond. McClellen made Fortress Monroe his base and advanced by way of the Peninsula; Johnston moved to join McGruder. Yorktown was held as long as Johnston thought advisable, and then the army was successfully withdrawn. The battle was fought at Williamsburg — the well calculated blow of Johnston was fierce and stunning, and his very deliberate retreat was no more interrupted. McClellan did not hesitate to claim this battle as a victory, but it was not so accorded him by the fairest critics at the North. The Confederates were not driven from a single position, but on the contrary, assumed the offensive, and at times held possession of all Hooker's artillery.

At the next battle, Seven Pines, Johnston was wounded and then unhorsed by a shell. He was taken to Richmond, and this ended his connection with the army of Northern Virginia. After five months of inactivity, on account of his wounds, he was ordered to the command of the Department of the West, including the States of Tennessee, Mississippi, South Carolina, and parts of Florida, Georgia, and North Carolina. Had the command been really delivered to him, it would have been the field for the employment of his gifts, but he soon learned the command was only in name. He asked for more definite work and was ordered to investigate General Braggs' command in Tennessee. There had been much complaint of Bragg's mismanagement, but Johnston was too generous to profit by his misfortune, and advised against the removal of Bragg. When orders came, putting him in his place, he asked to be relieved from the post on account of his health.

*   *   *   *

His next active service was to relieve Pemberton in Vicksburg. Johnston thought it inadvisable to keep such a large army inactive at Vicksburg, and so told the War Department. He urged Pemberton, time after time, to abandon Vicksburg and concentrate all his forces to fight Grant, before he (Grant) became too strong. His idea was always to save an army rather than a position, and if his advice had been followed, the immense loss to the South of this army and all its equipment, could have been averted. When he arrived it was too late to do any good, except by his good management save the army from the general wreck. He was then ordered to assume the command of the army of Tennessee. He found them disheartened and with no ordnance or materials.

The battle of Missionary Ridge, 1863, was the greatest disaster sustained by Confederate armies in pitched battle during the war. Nearly one-half of the guns, caissons, and munitions of the defeated army had been abandoned. Dalton had not been selected because of its defensive strength, but simply because the retreat from Missionary Ridge had ceased at that point. Johnston was sent to repair this disaster and did it very effectively, by reorganizing and reassuring the troops, so that when the campaign opened in the Spring, the poorest regiment he had was better than the best he had when he took charge.

The whole force was 42,856, while Sherman had 80,000 to oppose him. Then began that wonderful march, Johnston falling back, drawing Sherman's army after him, watching every move, never surprised, until he reached Atlanta, with Sherman's army just where he had planned to bring it. It seemed that he might reap the fruit of his labors, when he was struck the most treacherous blow of his whole life, and was ordered to turn over his command to General Hood. As usual, thinking more of his country than of his personal feelings, in this hour of humiliation, he gave General Hood all his plans. His worth is perhaps best estimated by the enemy. Sherman said, "At this critical moment, the Confederate Government rendered us most valuable service, being dissatisfied by the Fabian policy of General Johnston, it relieved him and General Hood was substituted to command the Confederate army."

After this he was given no command until February, 1865, when he was ordered to collect what had once been armies and oppose Sherman in North Carolina. Here he did wonders, but it was too late to effect the final result. The end seemed near at hand, and after Lee's surrender on April 9th, 1865, it was useless to prolong the struggle and sacrifice more precious lives. When he received word of the surrender of General Lee at Appomattox, he entered into correspondence with General Sherman, which led to the surrender of his army near Durham, North Carolina on April 26th, 1865.

When the war was over, he led a comparatively quiet life and tried to make a living for himself and wife. He served a term from Virginia in the Forty-Sixth Congress, and became United States Commissioner of Railways on April 2nd, 1885. His wife died in 1887 and he never seemed to recover from the blow. He attended the memorial exercises at Atlanta, Georgia, in the Spring of 1890 and received a grand ovation there. The old soldiers took the horses from his carriage and drew it themselves through the streets. The same year he attended the unveiling of the statute of Robert E. Lee in Richmond, and was greatly honored on this occasion. His health began to give away after the death of his wife. When General Sherman died he was selected as one of the pall-bearers and accepted the same as an honor. Here he contracted a cold from which he did not recover, dying March 21st, 1891, attended only by his brother-in-law, the lasting friend of his youth, Robert McLane.

When he died, great honor was paid to his memory throughout the South. His old foe, General Grant, said of him, "I have had nearly all the Southern Generals in high command in front of me, and Joe Johnston gave me more anxiety than any of the others." General Sherman always held him in high esteem and praised his tactics in war.

His soldiers said, at the end, "Farewell, old fellow, we privates loved you because you made us love ourselves."

Let us hold the names of our Confederate soldiers in grateful remembrance and love, and let the expanding millions of their countrymen renew and multiply their praise from generation to generation.

Sallie Yates Faison

General Nathan Bedford Forrest

On the 13th of July, 1821, in a rude cabin surrounded by poverty, and in a remote backwoods settle-
ment of Middle Tennessee, there was born a set of twins
— a boy and a girl. The boy grew to be a man who was so
different from the rest of men that he at once attracts our
attention.

This man was General Nathan Bedford Forrest.
The light first met his infant eyes through the cracks in the
chinking between the logs of hewn cedar, or through the
cracks of the roof made of boards held in place by heavy
poles instead of nails.

This humble cabin home was not larger than eighteen by twenty feet. It had one room below and a half-
room or "loft" overhead which was entered by a ladder.
One end of this building was nearly all given up to the
broad fireplace. There was no need of a window, for plenty of light came in through the cracks and down the low
squatty chimney.

Close by this cabin stood a log blacksmith shop
with bellows and forge, anvil, tongs, and hammer.

The owner of this shop was William Forrest, a man
more than six feet in height. He was an honorable man and
a law-abiding citizen.

For three generations the Forrests had belonged to a restless race of pioneers.

In 1806, Nathan Forrest with his family, among whom was William Forrest, then eight years old, came from North Carolina and settled in Tennessee not far from the present town of Gallatin, in Sumner county. Not satisfied with their surroundings, two years later they moved to the Duck River country in what was then Bedford county, Tennessee. Here William Forrest, the father of General N. B. Forrest, grew to manhood and learned the blacksmith's trade. He is said to have possessed great determination and to have exercised much influence in the community in which he lived.

It is said that General Forrest's love for his mother was one of the noblest traits of this great man's character.

There is an interesting story of how this mother controlled her boys. When the Civil War broke out in 1861, she resided upon her plantation near Memphis. One of the younger boys, then eighteen years of age, had for some months been employed as a clerk in a store in Memphis. He had just enlisted in the Confederate army. On a Friday afternoon he went to his mother's home dressed in a new suit of Confederate gray. His mother had some ideas which she was never willing to give up. One was that meal made from her own corn was better than any other meal. So every Saturday morning she would send one of the boys to mill with some corn.

As her son retired to his room that night she said, "Joseph, I want you to get up early in the morning and take some corn to mill." She did not take into consideration that he was living "away from home" and was a Confederate soldier. The young man went off to bed without saying anything, but determined that he would not soil his new soldier clothes by riding on a sack of meal.

The mother believed in getting up before daylight and having everything ready for work by the time it was light enough to see. The next morning everyone was called early, and all appeared at the table except Joseph. The old lady said to a Negro servant, "Tell Mr. Joseph to come to breakfast right away." She said as the servant went on the errand, "I am not going to have any city airs on this place." She then went on pouring the coffee for those at the table, when the Negro returned saying that Joseph said that he did not intend to go to mill, and she had as well send one of the niggers. The mother seemed dumbfounded at such impudence on the part of her son. Setting the half-filled cup and the coffee pot down, she arose from the table saying she would return in a few minutes. She went out into the yard, broke off three or four long peach tree switches, and went directly upstairs, pulled that eighteen-year-old warrior of hers out of bed and gave him such a thrashing as to cause him to remember it the rest of his life. She made him get up and put on his suit of old farm clothes he left at home when he became a "city chap." The horse was already at the gate and he was soon on his way to the mill. Her eyes flashing fire, she went back to the breakfast table saying, "Soldier or no soldier, my children will mind me as long as I live."

Another instance is given which goes to show her strong will. When they first settled in Mississippi, their nearest neighbor lived ten miles away. On one occasion Mrs. Forrest and her sister went on horseback to visit their neighbor. When they started home their friend gave them a basket containing several young chickens. Their trip home went well until they got within a mile of their cabin.

It was growing dark. Suddenly they heard a panther a few yards away. They knew the hungry beast had smelled the chickens. The horses became frightened and broke into a run. Mrs. Forrest's sister shouted back to her to drop the basket of chickens and let the panther have them, which would stop it.

Mrs. Forrest was not that sort of a woman. She did not intend to give up her chickens. Just as they reached the river the hungry panther made a leap striking Mrs. Forrest on the shoulder with its front paw and the horse with its hind foot. The horse plunged forward and the hold of the panther was torn loose. The screams of the women soon brought Bedford Forrest to the rescue. The fearless determination of this youth was shown as soon as his mother had been made comfortable. Young Forrest took his flintlock rifle and started to the door to call his dogs. His mother asked him where he was going. He said, "Mother, I am determined to kill that beast." She tried to persuade him not to go into the woods at that dark hour, but to wait till daylight. He said he was going while the scent was fresh and the dogs could follow the trail. So out into the darkness he went. The hounds picked up the trail and followed it until midnight. He soon saw he would be unable to keep up with the dogs so he cut a grapevine and tied it to the neck of one of the oldest dogs and held fast to the end of it. At times the other dogs would be out of hearing but the captive dog followed on. After a while he heard the baying of the pack which told him they had treed the panther. It was too dark for him to see the beast so he waited patiently till daylight. Then he saw it snarling at the dogs with its white teeth. The young huntsman taking steady aim sent a bullet through its heart and it fell dead to the ground.

* * * *

At the age of sixteen, by the death of his father, young Forrest was left to support his mother and family as best he could on a small farm. As he was almost the sole dependency of his mother and the children he would labor hard all day in the field and then at night sit up and work till very late making buckskin leggings and shoes and coon skin caps for the younger brothers. With these surroundings even the scantiest opportunities for an education were denied him, though he provided liberally for the education of his brothers and sisters.

It is a question as to whether or not he ever went to school. Free schools were unknown and the pay was so small that those who were capable of teaching could not be induced to do it.

We know from his spelling and talking he had but very little education. He spelled "headquarters" "hedquarters and "her" "hir."

He always said "betwixt" for "between," and "fetch" for "bring." He used the word "mout" for "might," and "fit" for "fight." He keenly felt the need of education and once remarked, "No one ever knows the embarrassment I labor under when thrown in the company of educated people."

Although he lacked school education yet his contact with business men and his reading of newspapers kept him thoroughly versed as to the times. This practical education and common sense always made him master of the situation. He had a great talent for mathematics. He had no training whatever yet he could solve the most difficult problems in Algebra, Geometry, and Trigonometry if some one would read the rule to him. He remained on the farm with his mother until he was twenty-one years of age. By this time he had shown so much business ability that his uncle living in Northern Mississippi offered him an interest in his business. In this he made quite a little fortune. He afterwards went into business in Memphis, Tennessee. He soon became able to purchase a large plantation and at the outbreak of the Civil War he was one of the wealthiest planters in Tennessee.

On the 25th of April, 1845, he married Miss Mary Montgomery, a lady of excellent family, refined and educated. She devoted her life to her husband and family. General Forrest's devotion to his wife was very deep. It is said that he almost worshiped her. She was very quiet and firm, yet sympathetic. She could control her husband with a word even when his temper was at its highest.

The manner in which he first met the young lady who afterward became his wife is quite interesting. As he was riding along a country road one day he came upon a vehicle stalled in a mudhole. As he came near he saw it contained two ladies. He also saw two men sitting on their horses nearby and making no effort to help the unfortunate women. Forrest dismounted, waded through the mud and water and carried them from the vehicle across the mud. He then put his shoulder to the wheel and soon had the vehicle out of the mudhole. He was so angry at the two men who had not offered to help the ladies that he told them if they did not leave there at once he would give them both such a thrashing as they would never forget.

Forrest introduced himself and asked permission of the ladies to call and make their acquaintance. He called and we know the result.

General Forrest was a very handsome man, six feet tall and weighed about 180 pounds. He was dignified in manner. He was very neat in personal appearance. He could not bear to leave papers scattered on the floor or ashes on the hearth. He would frequently take the broom and use it himself.

The tenderness of the stern warrior was shown in his fondness for children. Many times when in the homes of his friends he seemed to take little interest in conversing with the older people but spent most of the time in playing with the children.

When in camp if there was ever a time when he could absent himself he would go to the houses in the neighborhood where there were children, with whom he would frolic with as much joy as if he were a child again. In the midst of a desperate fight, when he seemed to have lost all thought except that of inflicting death, as he passed by a house he saw a woman stupefied with fright, standing with five or six children in direct range of the firing. Touched by her distress, he turned aside from the terrible struggle to order one of his staff to lead the mother and little ones to a place of safety.

General Forrest was a thorough believer in Christianity and had the most profound respect for religion. He always had preaching at his headquarters on Sunday if there was a minister at hand. He always had prayers in his tent at night. He had the profoundest disgust for profanity. Bishop Payne was one day in General Forrest's headquarters when one of the officers swore in the presence of the Bishop. Forrest could hardly contain himself at such outrageous conduct. He said to one standing close by, "If you think it ought to be done, I'll kick that hog out of the tent."

On an expedition a Chaplain of the Federal army was captured. When he learned he was to be sent to General Forrest's headquarters he was very much distressed as he had heard so much of this fierce fighter. When he entered the headquarters General Forrest asked him to be seated. A little later supper was announced and the Chaplain was asked to share the meal. When all were seated the Chaplain was almost shocked to hear General Forrest reverently say, "Parson, will you please ask the blessing." The next morning Forrest gave him an escort through his lines. When he told him good-bye he humorously said, "Parson, I would keep you here to preach for us if you were not needed so much more by the sinners on the other side."

He never started on an expedition but that he had the men drawn up in line and with the heads of all uncovered the Chaplain prayed the blessing of God on them.

Military Career

As to his military career General Forrest is the most remarkable man the Civil War developed and the greatest fighter of which the world has any record.

Without education and without any knowledge of war gotten from what others had done, he put into use the tactics and strategy of the most famous Generals in history. It had been said that he was born a soldier. If he had been afforded the advantages of a military education and training there is no question but that he would have been the greatest man in the Civil War.

One reason for his great success in the war was his spirit of devotion to the cause for which he was fighting. To the success of this cause he freely offered his fortune and his life.

When the Confederacy was unable to furnish him with supplies and arms, his private fortune was used for this purpose. On one expedition into West Tennessee he spent some twenty thousand dollars of his money to purchase supplies. His devotion to the cause led him to permit his only child, a mere lad, to quit college in order that he might serve in the war with his father. In a battle the boy was wounded and carried to the rear. As soon as it was possible his father went to see how dangerously he was hurt. When he was told that the boy was not seriously hurt, he ordered him to mount his horse and continue in the fight. This the plucky boy gladly did.

The greatest thing about General Forrest was his self-possession. Excitement never found a place in his calm mind. He was able to reason calmly and rapidly, no matter how serious the questions before him. On the battlefield, the unexpected thing always happens. Even at such times his presence of mind never failed him.

In addition to this calm and ready mind was a native cunning which always gave him the advantage over his foe.

On one occasion he was out with a small brigade of untrained men and he wished the enemy to think he had a large number of followers. So he had some of the Union sympathizers arrested and placed under guard. He got a number of drums which he caused to be beaten at all hours of the day and night. He had his troops marched by in sight of these prisoners. When these troops passed by and out of sight, they returned by another route, mounted their horses and filed by as cavalry over the same road which they had just passed. These prisoners were then permitted to escape. Of course, just as General Forrest intended, they went back to the headquarters of the commander and reported the great strength of the Confederate force.

At many places in the official report by the Federal commanders we can find Forrest's Cavalry reported many times larger than the number he ever had. This shows how well he could deceive his foe.

He was a very active man. His restless nature would not allow him to remain in camp longer than was necessary to rest his men and shoe his horses. He was always on the move and never satisfied unless he was whipping somebody.

He said, "War means fighting, and fighting means killing," and when the enemy were not hunting him, he was hunting them. If ever a man had a charmed life such was his. The assassin's bullet, the gun and sabre of the open fight failed to touch him. He was in more than one hundred battles and had twenty-seven horses shot from under him.

On one occasion his horse had carried him so far into the line of the Union forces before he could check him and turn to retreat that the soldiers rushed forward and attempted to surround and capture or kill him. They fired at him from all sides, shouting, "Shoot that man," "Knock him off his horse." So close were they at one time that one infantryman pushed his musket almost against Forrest's side and fired. The ball entered just above the left hip and lodged against the spinal column.

His horse though mortally shot, leaped from his rider's assailants and General Forrest with pistol in hand opened a way through which he spurred his horse and fled. It was many weeks before he recovered from this severe wound. The noble steed that had done such great service in this trying experience died from his wounds the next day.

An interesting anecdote is told showing the esteem in which Forrest was held by the people. As his army was retreating one day, an old lady ran out of her house to the gate and urged him to turn back and fight. As he rode on without stopping, she shook her fist at him and cried, "Oh, you great big, cowardly rascal, I only wish old Forrest were here; he would make you fight."

General Forrest was very brave himself and had no patience with a coward. One day during the thickest of the fight he saw one of his men running without hat or gun. In an instant Forrest seized him, threw him to the ground and while the bullets were whistling around him, gave the man a severe thrashing with a stick. Every soldier knew it was expected of him to fight to the death if it became necessary, and knew that General Forrest had no mercy for a coward. On one occasion he shot the color-bearer for stampeding. At another time he did the same thing to stop some panic-stricken Confederates.

The battle of Okolona was a very sad one for General Forrest. It was here his brother was killed. His grief was overpowering when he realized the brother, who on account of his father's death, had been tenderly reared and carefully educated, was dying. Although he was in hot pursuit of the enemy, he for a moment seemed to forget the great responsibility of his position as Commander. He dismounted, picked up his dying brother and held him in his arms as he would a child until his lifeblood was spent. The rough soldier kissed his dead brother tenderly, with tears streaming from his eyes, laid him gently on the ground, took one last look, and then the look of grief gave way to one of fierceness. He sprang to his horse shouting to his bugler, "Blow the charge," and swept on ahead of his men after the fleeing enemy. It was not long until he came up with them and they turned and renewed the battle. The General, maddened by the death of his brother, fought as he had never fought before. Soon his horse was killed under him, and he mounted another, belonging to one of the escorts who had just ridden up. In a few minutes this horse was also killed. Forrest killed three men with his sword in this terrible fight before the Federals yielded and fled from the field.

General Forrest was a desperate fighter and fought with reckless courage. His plan of fighting was to have his men dismount from their horses and mix with the enemy. He was always in the front leading his men and not in the rear spying out the field with a glass. He led the charge in some of the bloodiest and most hotly contested battles during the war.

His record during the war makes him first of the cavalry leaders, and one of the half-dozen great soldiers of our country.

When the great war was over and all his black hair was silvered, his heart, too, was subdued; he became very conscious of the Unseen Power that had spared him through so many battles.

His faithful friend, Major Charles W. Anderson, visited him a few months before his death. He at once noticed a softness of expression and a mildness of manner which he had not noticed in the trying times of war.

General Forrest, as if reading his thoughts, said, "Major, I am not the man you were with so long and knew so well. I hope I am a better man now than then. I have been and am trying to lead another kind of life. I have for some time been a member of the Cumberland Presbyterian Church. My wife has been praying for me all these years, and I feel now that through her prayers my life has been spared and I passed safely through so many dangers."

Although he received the tenderest and most skilled attention, the dread disease which was destroying his life could not be stayed, and at his home in Memphis, on October 29th, 1877, he died at the age of fifty-six.

His death created sadness throughout the entire country. Many of those against whom he had fought in battle united with the South to pay tribute to his memory, and thousands upon thousands of high and low degree followed his body to the grave.

General Albert Sidney Johnston

Boyhood and School Days

Albert Sidney Johnston was born on the 2nd day of February, 1803, in the village of Washington, Mason county, Kentucky. He was the youngest son of Doctor John Johnston, a physician, and one of the earliest settlers of that town. His mother was a Miss Harris, the daughter of Edward Harris, an old settler who had emigrated from Massachusetts. Mr. Harris was a good man, and had great respect for the Sabbath. He had been a Revolutionary soldier, and was appointed military store keeper and postmaster at Washington, Kentucky by President George Washington. A letter to the Postmaster-General can be seen now in which he resigned the position of postmaster, because some new postal arrangement required him to open the mail on Sunday, which he did not think was right. The letter plainly shows him to have been an educated and thoughtful man.

His wife, General Johnston's mother, is said to have been a beautiful lady of fine intellect, and sterling worth. She had received a most excellent training from her wise and good father, which she transmitted to her sons.

Doctor Johnston was a skilled physician. He knew the value of education, and gave his children the best the times afforded.

The boyhood of Albert Sidney Johnston was very simple and without show. He was reared in the country and at a time when the habits of all classes were plain. Captain Wilson Duke, one of Johnston's close friends of his youth, used laughingly to tell how he tore off his ruffled shirt collar and hid his shoes on the road to school, from fear of Albert Johnston's ridicule.

Young Johnston had a very high temper, but he had judgment and power of self-control that always held him in check. His eldest sister said of him that, when a boy, he was fearless and impetuous, but kind, affectionate, and just.

He was a handsome, proud, manly, earnest, and self-reliant boy. He was distinguished for his courage in boyhood. He was a born gentleman, and was as far from being a bully as any boy in the world, yet he was one whom the bullies left alone.

General Johnston told an anecdote of his early boyhood from which we can draw many valuable lessons. Playing marbles "for keeps" was a favorite sport of his school-boy days; and he was so skilled and successful a player that he had won a whole jar full of marbles. It was at this time he made up his mind to win all of the marbles in town, in the State, and eventually in the world. Filled with enthusiasm, he began to cast about for the means and concluded the wisest thing for him to do would be to bury them as he won them. He buried his jar very secretly, reserving only marbles enough "to begin life on." He was very successful and added daily to his store. Only one competitor stood against him who seemed to have an inexhaustible supply of marbles. At last he too succumbed and young Johnston went with a jar larger than the first to add to his spoil. To his dismay he found his treasure gone. The boy who held out so long had watched him where he hid his treasure, robbed him, and then staked and lost all his ill-gotten gains. The second jar contained the same marbles as the first. General Johnston said that he felt the lesson a distinct rebuke and his plan soon vanished.

In school Johnston was a brilliant student. Mr. John P. Morton, of Louisville, who sat next him in class, says, "He was conspicuous for always knowing his lessons." In 1822 his brother, Josiah S. Johnston, then a member of Congress from Louisiana, procured for him an appointment to the Military Academy at West Point.

His sister tells an interesting story of him. He had a beautiful riding horse, which he thought of selling before leaving for West Point. As the time approached for his departure he would turn his favorite out of the stable and watch his graceful movements as he enjoyed the freedom of the pasture. When the time came for him to go, he gave him to his sister, saying, "I cannot sell that horse into hands where he would be badly treated; but you will treat him well." He always treated his horse and dog with the kindest consideration. Often he would walk and lead his horse, when it had become tired.

In West Point, Johnston made a good record. In June, 1826, he was graduated, ranking eighth in his class. When the final examination came he felt satisfied that he had mastered everything in the course but two problems. The first thing he was called upon to do, was to discuss one of these problems. On this he failed, hoping for better luck the next time; but to his dismay the next question was the other neglected problem. He again failed. He was ordered to take his seat. He felt that his reputation was at stake, so he briefly stated to the professor that these were the only problems in the whole course he could not solve. He was sternly ordered to take his seat, which he did. If the matter had ended here, he would have failed and lost his commission; but as soon as the class was dismissed he sent a letter to the examiners stating the facts and challenging the most rigid test.

Finally he was given another long and searching examination. In spite of the reduction on account of the previous failure and of skill in drawing, he was graded eighth in his class.

As a Soldier

On account of his high rank in his class he was entitled to select the arm of the service he preferred — whether the artillery or the infantry. Had a cavalry corps then existed, he would have entered it; but between the artillery and the infantry, he chose the latter. He selected the infantry because it was employed in more active service than the artillery. He was assigned to the Second Infantry to take effect on July 1st, 1826. He left the Military Academy with kind feelings to his classmates, and a high regard for the institution.

Soon after this appointment, he was offered the position of aid to General Scott, and from his own judgment refused it, saying that although much gratified to have been mentioned by General Scott, he felt that the life of inactivity in a large city did not accord with his views, and that he preferred to go to the far West and enter at once upon the active duties of his profession. For the refusal of this offer extended as a kindness, General Scott for a long time regarded Mr. Johnston with unusual coolness.

Johnston was assigned to "The Sixth" as Second Lieutenant under General Henry Atkinson. This was considered the "crack" regiment; so he at once proceeded rejoicing to its headquarters at Jefferson Barracks. The Barracks was near enough to St. Louis to allow the young officer to mingle in its gay society. It was here at a ball that Lieutenant Johnston met for the first time Miss Henrietta Preston. It was not long until a mutual love prompted an engagement, and they were married on January 20th, 1829.

There were many points of resemblance between Lieutenant Johnston and his wife. A friend, who knew them well, said that he never knew two people more alike in character. They were often mistaken for brother and sister. Mrs. Johnston's manner was full of dignity and ease. She had a firm yet gentle temper. She was very fond of poetry and wrote it with ease and feeling. She was much beloved by her family and friends. Her husband said, it was impossible to have felt her influence and afterwards to cherish low views; that to her he owed the wish to be truly great. For three years the married life of this happy couple was simple and uneventful in their home at Jefferson Barracks. But these happy and peaceful days were soon to be disturbed by the rude note of war.

The Black Hawk War broke out in 1832. To this war Johnston went and gave noble service. The time he was away in this war was a season of sore trial to his wife. She said that on one occasion during this time their daughter, supposed to be dead, was by God's mercy restored to them. The child was in her coffin; but a lady thought she saw signs of life and by a hot bath and other remedies re-

stored her, and she still lives. A letter Mrs. Johnston wrote
her mother gives us an idea of her feelings at this time. In
this letter she said, "Between physical fatigue and mental
anxiety for my children, for you and for my good husband,
I am scarcely myself. I try to be cheerful. God alone
knows how it will end. I have been busy today making up
flannel for my husband, and writing to him."

When Johnston returned to Jefferson Barracks he
found Mrs. Johnston broken in health. Her failing health
made her long for the quiet of a permanent home. So she
urged her husband to resign from the army. Although he
regretted very much to give up the army life, yet to gratify
the cherished wish of her heart, he did so, and bought a
farm near St. Louis. It was sincerely hoped that her health
could be regained, but consumption had taken a deadly
hold of her constitution. Mr. Johnston devoted all of his
time to the care of his invalid wife, whom he tenderly
nursed until on the 12th of August, 1835, she died.

After the death of his wife, Mr. Johnston made the
home he prepared in anticipation of happiness his refuge
in affliction. He had left his children, who were so young
as to require female care, with their grandmother, Mrs.
Preston, at Louisville.

Mr. Johnston was in such great distress of mind
that he did not remain long on his farm. He heard the ap-
peals in behalf of Texas. He heard of the heroism and suffering of the emigrants from the United States and speed-
ily decided to help them. He enlisted as a private soldier,
and by his personal qualities, both physical and mental,
soon attained notice and rapidly rose through all the
grades to the command of the army, succeeding General
Felix Houston. General Houston was so angered by his
appointment, that he sent General Johnston a challenge to

fight a duel.

This challenge was immediately accepted and the next morning at seven o'clock was fixed for the hour of meeting. There were no dueling pistols to be found in the camp, so it was proposed to use General Houston's horse pistols. General Johnston was a poor shot with a pistol, while General Houston's unrivaled skill was well known. It is a wonder he did not select the sword, with which he would have had the advantage. General Houston's superior skill prevailed, and General Johnston fell, with a bullet through his hip. From this wound he lay for weeks at the point of death.

While in command of the Army of the Republic of Texas, General Johnston rescued a little girl and her brother from the Indians. The parents of the children were killed while walking with their children one Sunday afternoon. The babe was also killed, but the other two children, a girl of seven and a boy of five, were captured and held by the Indians.

General Johnston heard of the killing, followed the Indians, and overtook them near a thicket, where he scattered the red men and captured the children. On hearing the approach of the soldiers, the Indians pierced the boy in the side with a spear, and struck the girl on the head, leaving them for dead. The little girl soon revived and dragged her little brother from the bushes. She responded to the calls of the soldiers, and General Johnston took her up behind him on his horse after caressing her and soothing her sorrowing, frightened heart, and left her with a good minister and his family.

At fifteen years of age this child married the Rev. Orsenus Fisher, and Mrs. Rebecca J. Fisher is today the honored and beautiful, although aged, President of the Daughters of the Republic of Texas.

Little Rebecca Gilleland — Mrs. Fisher — always remained a close friend to General Johnston; the surviving wife of General Johnston sent to the Daughters of the Republic of Texas, because of their love for Mrs. Fisher, the helmet, sleeve, and sword of General Johnston which he wore at Shiloh. These are kept in a glass case in the Capitol Building, in the room of the Daughters of the Republic of Texas.

In 1838 he was made Secretary of War by President M.B. Lamar of the Republic of Texas, which position he held for two years.

When Texas had been annexed to the United States, and her disputed boundary brought on a war between Mexico and the United States, he was made Colonel of a Volunteer Regiment of Texas Rifles.

On October 3rd, 1843, Mr. Johnston was married to Miss Eliza Griffin, a lady of great beauty, talents, and accomplishments. It was his intention now to engage in agricultural pursuits. In partnership with a friend he purchased a farm of 4,428 acres in Texas. For this farm they paid $16,000, a price much too large. Mr. Johnston paid his part of this amount, but his friend became so involved in debt that he could not pay his part. He appealed to Mr. Johnston to buy his half of the farm, which he did. His friend was saved but he sacrificed himself.

The years between 1842 and 1846 were spent in the vain effort to pay for the farm. He remained on his farm until 1849, when President Taylor appointed him a pay-master. He served in this capacity for more than five years and made six tours riding over 4,000 miles each year

on the Indian frontier of Texas. He paid to the troops between $40,000 and $50,000 every four months.

He had to go from Austin, Texas, to New Orleans
to get this money. As he returned he went by steamer to
Galveston, thence by steamboat to Houston, and thence by
stage, a distance of one hundred and eighty-five miles, to
Austin. The journey was continued day and night for
about a week. In addition to perils by sea and yellow fever, the stage road had its dangers. There was great danger of robbery. The money was in gold and silver coin
packed in an iron chest and was always placed between
the feet of two guards who watched in turn from New
Orleans to Austin.

When on trips paying soldiers General Johnston's
bed was made of a buffalo robe and some blankets; and
two daily meals of cold bread, cold ham, and black coffee,
with an occasional bird or wild duck, shot by the road.

In 1855, President Pierce appointed him Colonel
of the Second Cavalry. He remained in command of this
regiment and this Department of Texas until 1857, when
he was ordered to the command of the expedition to restore order among the Mormons in Utah, who were in
open rebellion against the National Government. By the
successful manner in which he executed this delicate and
hazardous mission, he won just reputation for his energy
and wisdom, and in 1857 was made Brigadier-General. He
held this position till April 9th, 1861.

He viewed with grief the approaching conflict between the States. He was deeply attached to the government, and felt that its highest posts were within the reach
of his ambition, but when he heard of the secession of
Texas, he felt it was his duty to go with his State, and on

April 9th, 1861, he resigned his position in the army of the United States.

At this time he was in charge of the Department of the Pacific, stationed in California. It was a long journey from where he was to Richmond, Virginia, and it was September before he reached there. He at once tendered his service to the Confederate States of America, and was assigned to the command of the army of Tennessee.

This brave and true soldier had nearly completed his record for he was spared to do service for only a few months in the Confederate Army. At that early period of the war no Confederate Commander held higher place in the hopes and expectations of the Southern Army and people. What his record might have been, was lost to all time in his early death, on the first day of the battle of Shiloh, April 6th, 1862.

He met his death in leading a charge. Senator Isham G. Harris, of Tennessee, who was with him, gives the following account of his death:

I galloped to Colonel Statham only about two hundred yards distant, gave the order sent him and galloped back to the General, where a moment before I had left him. I rode up to his right side and said, "General, your order is delivered and General Statham is in motion," but as I was uttering the sentence, the General reeled from me in a manner that indicated he was falling from his horse. I put my left arm around his neck, grasped the collar of his coat, and righted him up in the saddle. I bent forward as I did so, and looking him in the face said, "General, are you wounded?" In a very deliberate and emphatic tone he answered, "Yes, and I fear seriously." At that moment I requested Captain Wickham to go with all possible speed for a surgeon, to send the first one he could find, but to proceed until he could find Dr. Yandell, the medical director, and bring him. The General's hold upon the rein relaxed, and it dropped from his hand, I supporting him with my left hand, gathered his rein with my right, in which I held my own, and guided both horses to a valley about one hundred and fifty yards in the rear. My impression is that he did not live more than thirty or forty minutes from the time he received his wound. His body was wrapped in a mantle to conceal his death from the army, and taken to Corinth, and thence to New Orleans, and placed in a vault, where it remained until January 24th, 1867, when it was taken to Galveston, Texas, for final burial.

General Johnston was a man to be loved, to be reverenced, and to be emulated. One who had known him most intimately writes, "He was gentle to women and children, tender to the weak and suffering, gracious to subordinates and dependants, just and magnanimous to equals and rivals, respectful to superiors and tolerant to all men."

No eulogy has been composed, no tribute has been rendered, giving more fitting expression to the lofty qualities that marked the illustrious dead, when living, than the following beautiful epitaph which was found pasted on a rough board attached to the tomb by a lady passing through the St. Louis Cemetery of New Orleans.

In Memoriam
by John S. Dimitry of New Orleans

Behind this stone is laid for a season A. S. Johnston, a General in the Army of the Confederate States, who fell at Shiloh, Tennessee, on the sixth day of April, eighteen hundred and sixty-two.

A man tried in many high offices and critical enterprises and found faithful in all.

His life was one long sacrifice of interest to conscience; and even that life on a woeful Sabbath, did he yield as a holocaust, at his country's need — not wholly understood was he while he lived; but in his death his greatness stands confessed, in a people's tears.

Resolute, moderate, clear of envy, yet not wanting in that finer ambition which makes men great and pure. In his honor impregnable; in his sublimity sublime. No country e'er had a truer son — no cause a nobler champion; no people a bolder defender; no principle a purer victim, than the dead soldier who sleeps here.

The cause for which he perished is lost, the people for whom he fought are crushed — the hopes in which he trusted are shattered; the flag he loved guides no more the charging lines.

But his fame consigned to the keeping of that time, which happily is not so much the tomb of virtue as its shrine, shall in years to come fire modest worth to noble ends.

In honor now our great captain rests; a bereaved people mourn him; the commonwealth proudly claims him, and history shall cherish him among those choice spirits who, holding their conscience unmixed with blame, have been in all conjunctions true to themselves, their people and their God.

Mrs. Joseph B. Dibrell

Fort Sumter

The first gun fired in a great war is always an event by which to mark time. In the war between the States all the Southern States were aroused to the necessity for action, but the nucleus about which the storm was to center was the little State of South Carolina.

On December 20th, 1860, the ordinance of secession was passed in Charleston, South Carolina by which the Palmetto State withdrew from the Union of States. Six days after this action on the part of South Carolina, at dead of night, Major Anderson and the United States troops garrisoned at Fort Moultrie on Sullivan's Island, South Carolina, moved over to Fort Sumter and there established themselves. This was done because the fort was a more secure place than Fort Moultrie.

This movement of Major Anderson in such unsettled times was really the first step in a declaration of war between the United States and the seceding States. Fort Sumter is about three miles from Charleston and in the mouth of her harbor, a mile equidistant from Fort Moultrie and Sullivan's Island on one side, and Fort Johnson and Morris Island on the other. The site had been ceded by the State of South Carolina to the United States Government for the general protection of all the States. It covered about two and a half acres. In form it was five sided, rising directly out of the water, and built on an artificial foundation of granite, sand and mud. Its wall was forty feet high and was of brick and concrete. In thickness it ranged from five to ten feet, and on the north, east, and west was pierced by three tiers of guns.

As soon as South Carolina separated from the Union, she demanded back the land ceded to the General Government, offering to pay for the fortifications upon it. President Buchanan refused to withdraw the United States troops from Fort Sumter, and sent the "Star of the West," a small ship, with troops to re-enforce the Fort. A few shots fired from Morris Island by the Confederates on January 9th, 1861, caused her to turn back and she returned to New York.

After the establishment of the Southern Confederacy in Montgomery, February, 1861, three Commissioners were sent to Washington to negotiate with the United States for friendship and peace. Mr. Lincoln would not receive these men officially; however they waited a long while in Washington, hoping to arrange for a peaceful surrender of Fort Sumter to the Confederates. But on April 8th, the Governor of South Carolina, Mr. Pickens, heard that a United States fleet was on its way to strengthen Fort Sumter. This was a declaration of war in truth and General Beauregard, who was in command of the Confederate forces around Charleston, received orders from the Confederate Government at Montgomery to demand the evacuation of the fort. This he did, notifying Major Anderson that if it was not evacuated he would bombard it. Finally at 4:30 a.m. on April 12th, 1861, the Confederates began the bombardment, which they kept up for thirty-three hours, when the United States flag was lowered on the fort and on April 14th surrender was made to the Confederates. The United States garrison was allowed to salute their flag and were then taken out and conveyed to the United States gunboats waiting outside the bar and carried to New York. There were none killed in this engagement except two United States soldiers in the Fort, and they were killed by the bursting of their own cannon in firing the salute to their own flag.

Fort Sumter was now in the possession of the Confederates and was to live a stormy life. It suffered three principle and eight minor bombardments by the United States troops, and forty-six thousand projectiles were hurled at it during the war. Thirty-five hundred tons of metal were hurled at it, and twenty-four hundred tons hit it, but the Confederates held their fort. For one hundred and fifty-seven days and one hundred and sixteen nights it was under a *steady* fire, and for one hundred and twenty-three days an occasional fire, making in all two hundred and eighty days under fire.

In the beginning it was an artillery post with five hundred and fifty men and eighty guns. An attack was made on it April, 1863, when nine United States vessels took part and bombarded it for two hours and twenty minutes, but they withdrew after this time with five out of the nine vessels disabled; one, the *Keokuk* sunk in the harbor the next day, and in five days they withdrew from the waters about Sumter. The guns on the *Keokuk* were afterwards raised by the Confederates after being abandoned by the United States authorities, and were used in the defense of Charleston in the later part of the war.

The great bombardment of the fort occurred in August, 1863, and lasted sixteen days, but it did not surrender. The authorities decided that it could no longer be used as an artillery post, so Colonel Rhett withdrew his artillery, and Major Stephen Elliott took charge with about three hundred and thirty-two infantrymen, on September, 1863, and right well did they hold their post.

The second great bombardment occurred from October 26 to December 6th, 1863, lasting forty-one days. During this attack six times was the flag shot away from its staff, and six times with dauntless courage was it replaced; eighteen thousand shots were fired at plucky little Sumter during this attack, and when the demand was made for her to surrender, Major Elliott's reply would be, "Come and take her." Finally Major Elliott was promoted to Colonel, then Brigadier-General, and sent to Virginia, and Captain John Mitchell, a brave young Irishman, was put in charge of the three hundred men and the plucky little fort.

The fort was now in pretty good order for defense, and by means of sand bags, logs, wires, ropes, and various engineering devices the fort was constantly repelling night attacks from the United States troops, both from their boats and their land batteries along the neighboring islands. Captain John Mitchell was killed while reconnoitering in July, 1864, and Thomas A. Huguenin was put in command. After September 1st, 1864, there was no firing on the fort. It stood silently garrisoned, on the watch but unsurrendered!

Finally in February, 1865, Sherman with his seventy thousand men passed through South Carolina scattering death, fire, destruction and ruin in his path, when orders came from the Confederate Government to evacuate Fort Sumter. For twelve months after it had been demolished as an artillery post, and after the entire coast of South Carolina had been abandoned to the United States troops, little Sumter had stood unsurrendered. *It was never surrendered,* but on the night of February 17th, 1865, sadly her brave defenders spiked her guns. Gallant little Sumter whom they had defended with their best brain, blood, and courage, must be abandoned, and in perfect order the three hundred brave men silently left the fort, stepped in the boats and were landed in the city of Charleston, and thus after five hundred and sixty-seven days of siege, "Sumter's sword was sheathed in Charleston Bay."

Mary B. Poppenheim

General Pierre G.T Beauregard

General Beauregard was born of French parents in New Orleans, May 28th, in the year 1818. His parents, especially his mother, were of French nobility, which accounts for his long Christian name: Pierre Gustave Toutant Beauregard. At home he was called "Toot," and at school and among familiar acquaintances he was known as "Gus."

His father was a soldier in the French army. As he was the son of a trained soldier and reared in a military home, it is easy to account for the statement that General Beauregard was a natural-born soldier. He had many qualities of mind and character shown in his childhood that go to make a good soldier.

In the first place he was a good student in school, obedient and manly — two things that belong to every great soldier. Another trait that distinguished General Beauregard was his great determination. An incident occurred in his boyhood which shows both his determination and self-respect, and, certainly, no General of the Civil War commanded more respect of friend and foe than did General Beauregard.

When about nine years old he was spending a day at the home of an aunt in the neighborhood of his father's estate, where had assembled several relatives and many comrades of his own age. Among the gentlemen present was one noted for teasing. He had taken young Beauregard to task and was attempting to make a target of him for the amusement of others. While he was enjoying his practical jokes, young Beauregard, his patience exhausted, suddenly seized a stick that lay near at hand, and so violently and rapidly assaulted his tormentor that he forced him to retreat to an outhouse close by, where he stood guard over the gentleman until an apology had been made.

When a little over ten years of age he was thought to be well prepared to become a communicant of the Catholic Church, which is a very sacred and solemn occasion. All in readiness, the little boy, deeply serious, lighted candle in hand, as is the custom among Roman Catholics, was advancing up the aisle, when the roll of a drum sounded through the church. Gustave hesitated, looked toward his anxious family kneeling in their pew, the drum rolled again, and the boy turned and dashed out after it, and his act of religion was deferred to a later period.

At the age of eleven he was taken to New York where he remained four years under the instruction of Messrs. Peugnet. At sixteen he entered the Military Academy of West Point, where four years later, July 1, 1838, he graduated second in a class of forty-five, and was at once appointed Second Lieutenant of Engineers, United States Army. In 1846-47, according to plans drawn up by Captain Barnard and himself, he directed the fortification works at the city of Tampico, Mexico.

Young Beauregard won distinguished honors at West Point as being the best student in the record of the school in Geography, Surveying, and Map-Making.

The position of Engineer in an army is an important one. He maps out for the commander every hill, valley, river, forest, mountain, and road in the whole country. Indeed the success of a great campaign very often depends upon the knowledge of a country where the fighting is to take place.

General Beauregard and General McPherson of the Federal Army rank as the greatest Military Engineers of the United States.

In March, 1847, he joined General Winfield S. Hancock against the City of Mexico; he distinguished himself at the siege of Vera Cruz, and in several bold reconnaissances before the battle of Cerro Gordo and in most of the engagements in Mexico. The strongest proof of his genius in engineering matters was shown in the Mexican War, when in opposition to most of the general officers present and others of high authority, he advised an attack by the Western approaches of Mexico. His idea was accepted and was successful. Lieutenant Beauregard was twice wounded in the brilliant assault on the Carita de Belen. He was promoted to be Captain for gallant conduct. He remained in the service and was until 1860 stationed in Louisiana and in charge of the building of the Custom House in New Orleans. He had been appointed to the charge of the Military Academy at West Point in 1860, but only held it a few days, as war was threatening. Louisiana seceded January 26th, 1861. Major Beauregard resigned from the United States Army, and on March 1st became Brigadier-General in the Confederate States Army. General Beauregard was assigned to Charleston, South Carolina, to prepare that city for defence. It was by his order that the first gun in defense of the South was fired April 12th, 1861.

Shortly after four o'clock in the dull gray morning of Friday, April 12th, 1861, signs of excitement and agitation were seen among the citizens of Charleston, South Carolina. Although earlier than most persons are astir, yet streams of people poured through the streets leading to the wharves and battery. Fashionable ladies, and anxious workmen, all looked toward the sea watching tiny wreaths of smoke curling upwards from one point of view on the right and another on the left, James and Sullivan Islands. Soon a dull heavy sound fell upon the ear, the whiz of bullets, heavy cannonading. The Stars and Stripes floated still over Fort Sumter. The Government of the Confederate States had hoped that the little garrison would yield without resistance, as the fort was on South Carolina soil. The letters and messages exchanged between Major Anderson, U.S.A., and General Beauregard, are models of courtesy, courage, and determination. General Beauregard offered to transport Major Anderson and his command to any United States port he might select, with all company arms and property and private property and permit him to salute his flag on leaving it. To this Major Anderson would not consent, but as the messengers were leaving he said, even if the fort was not battered down, his command would soon be starved out. After more parleying, every effort on the part of the Confederate Government was made to avoid bloodshed As General Beauregard learned, ships were at hand to enter Charleston harbor and relieve Major Anderson. In spite of warnings, it was ordered that fire be opened on the fort to which Fort Sumter at once replied, and the affair became a regular engagement, though no casualties resulted.

The Confederate troops cheered the little garrison for its plucky action and hooted at the United States ships lying inactive outside. The fort surrendered to the Confederates the same day, and although it was not usual to permit it, the gallant garrison were allowed to salute their flag upon leaving it. Major Anderson and his command were sent out to the Federal ships instead of to prison and before sunset the Confederate flag floated over Sumter. General Beauregard considered it madness for the enemy's fleet to try to attack Charleston from the sea. Indeed his engineering and military genius, which is considered only next to that of Vauban, the great French Engineer, made Charleston impregnable from the sea. She was only captured by a combined land and naval attack. Shortly after the fall of Sumter, General Beauregard was placed in command of forces in Virginia, and fought the first battle of Manassas, or Bull Run, July 21st, 1861. He was, very late in the action, superseded in command by General Joseph E. Johnson, his superior officer, who however allowed Beauregard to conduct the engagement according to his previous plans. The Southern troops were brave and devoted, but were volunteers and not fully disciplined. For this or other reasons, the fleeing Federal troops were not pursued all the way to Washington, and it is still thought by many that the Confederate troops did not reap the full fruits of their victory, which was complete. The Union soldiers were supplied with everything that should or might be used or enjoyed. Many persons had driven out from Washington to enjoy the sight of the rout of the Southern forces. Champagne was provided in abundance as well as other delicacies. The bloody field of Manassas showed the people of the North what they had to expect, and alas, preparations were begun which, too, surely showed the great resources of the Federal Government.

On January, 1862, General Beauregard was called to the Department of the West, and second in command to General Albert Sidney Johnston at the battle of Shiloh. The first day, April 6th, the Confederate forces were successful, but General Johnston was killed. General Bureaguard was in bad health, and fresh and superior forces being brought up by the Federal Generals, the Confederates withdrew in good order.

April the 7th, General Beauregard issued an appeal to churches and citizens to contribute their bells to be melted for cannon. This met with free response. At an auction sale in New Orleans, after the fall of that city, there is an item of 418 bells, one having painted on it, "General Beauregard from Baptist Church of Durhamville, Tenn."

General Beauregard withdrew for a few weeks in an endeavor to recuperate his health. In August, 1862, he returned to active service, and in September, 1863, was again in Charleston, where his measures of defense for that city and neighborhood called forth encomiums at home and abroad.

On May 7th, 1864, he commanded in a terrific combat at Petersburg, Virginia, and in October was assigned to the Mississippi, Georgia, Alabama, and East Louisiana Department. He surrendered with General Joseph E. Johnston, April 20th, 1865, and returned to his home near New Orleans, where he took up the peaceful life of a planter, advocating and practicing loyalty to the oath taken to the United States Government. He resumed the practice of engineering and became President of a street railway company.

General Beauregard was twice married, first to Miss Marie Laure Villere, by whom he had three children,

René and Henri, Major and Captain in the Confederate Army, and Laure. His second wife was Miss Caroline Deslondes, who died in 1864, while her husband was absent in the field.

General Beauregard was a man of medium height, very black eyes and dark hair and complexion, his cheek bones were high, and his chin square and determined. His was a most soldierly figure, a pure type of the highest class of Louisiana Creole, i.e., a native of Louisiana of French and Spanish descent. In manners he was quiet and reserved and most courteous. His education was thorough and he was master of both the French and English languages. His character was high and he pursued his modest way, devoted to his family and near friends, who returned his affection with loyal attachment. He died in New Orleans, February 20th, 1893.

A war incident of interest is that connected with the adoption of a battle flag of the one with red ground and blue cross. At one period at the battle of Manassas or Bull Run, General Beauregard was anxiously expecting reinforcements, and dreading that the enemy might secure the same. The General fixed his field glasses upon a distant body of troops advancing. The day was still and the folds of the flag drooped about the staff. The Confederate flag at this time was three bars — red, white, and red — and a blue union with a circle of stars. Moments of anguish passed when suddenly a puff of wind threw the Stars and Bars to the breeze, and the Confederate troops were at hand.

Designs were called for, and one from Louisiana was accepted. It was a square flag, red field with blue St. Andrew's cross, carrying on each arm three stars and one in the center. The Misses Cary of Baltimore and Virginia made three flags from their silk dresses, and the one given to General Beauregard was saved by being sent to Havana, and is now in Memorial Hall in New Orleans.

A monument to General Beauregard is about to be erected in New Orleans, in which city one of the public schools bears his name.

Mrs. D. A. S. Vaught

The Young Hero Sam Davis

Sam Davis is the youngest yet one of the true heroes of the Civil War. He was born October 6th, 1842, near Smyrna, Tennessee.

In the garden of the home where he was born is a beautiful monument erected by a loving father. On this monument are these words: "He laid down his life for his country. He suffered death on the gibbet rather than betray his friends and his country."

When the war broke out, Sam Davis was attending a military school in Nashville, Tennessee.

He enlisted in the Confederate Army as a private soldier. His record was so good that he was soon chosen a member of a company of scouts under Captain Shaw.

These scouts slept in thickets and were fed by ladies, who would take them food at night and tell them all they knew about the movements of the Federal forces. Of all the company Sam Davis was one of the coolest and bravest. These scouts had been told when they started on this dangerous work that but few of them might return; that they would probably be captured and killed.

About November 20th, 1863, with reports as complete as was possible to procure, and a note from Captain Shaw, Sam Davis started on his most perilous journey through Federal to Confederate lines. He undertook this journey wearing Confederate gray with pride and independence.

The Union Army of 16,000 men occupied Pulaski, Tennessee, and surrounding country. The commander of this army had been much disturbed by the successful work of these scouts and he determined to stop them at whatever cost.

They captured Sam Davis with these reports and Captain Shaw's note on his person. They also found in his saddle seat some maps and descriptions of some fortifications at Nashville, Tennessee. He was captured under the bluff at Bainbridge (Alabama) Ferry, on the Tennessee River. When he realized he must surrender he threw his package of papers as far as he could into the river, but a Federal officer followed them as they floated down the river and got them. He was taken to Pulaski, Tennessee, and placed in jail. The next morning he was taken to the headquarters of the Federal General. He was taken into the private office, and was told that it was a very serious charge brought against him; that he was a spy, and from what was found upon his person he had accurate information in regard to the army. The General demanded him to tell where he got this information. He told Sam Davis that he was a young man, and did not realize the danger he was in. Up to that time he had said nothing, but then he replied in the most respectful manner, "General, I know the danger I am in and I am willing to take the consequences."

He was asked then to give the name of the person from whom he obtained the information, but he firmly declined to do so. He was told that he would have to be tried for his life, and, from the proof he would be condemned; that there was no chance for him unless he gave the source of his information. He replied, "I know that I will have to die, but I will not tell where I got the information, and there is no power on earth that can make me tell. You are doing your duty as a soldier and I am doing mine. If I have to die, I do so feeling that I am doing my duty to my God and my country."

The Federal General pleaded with and urged him with all his power to give him some chance to save his life, for he saw he was a most admirable young fellow. To whom Sam replied, "It is useless to talk to me. I do not intend to tell. You can kill me or do anything you like, but I will not betray a trust placed in me."

He thanked the General for the interest he had taken in him, and he was sent back to prison. A court-martial to try him was at once called. He was tried and sentenced to be hanged the next day, Friday, November 27th, 1863, between the hours of 10 a.m. and 2 p.m.

He was at once informed of the sentence. He was surprised at the humiliating punishment. He expected to be shot and never thought they would hang him, but he determined to meet his fate bravely. That night he wrote the following letter to his mother:

Pulaski, Tennesseee
Nov. 26th, 1863.

Dear Mother: O, how painful it is to write to you. I have got to die tomorrow to be hanged by the Federals. Mother, do not grieve for me. I must bid you good-bye forever. Mother, I do not fear to die. Give my love to all.

Your son, Samuel Davis.

P.S. Mother, tell the children all to be good. I wish I could see you all once more, but I never will any more. Mother and father, do not forget me. Think of me when I am dead, but do not grieve for me. It will not do any good. Father, you can send after my body if you wish to do so. It will be at Pulaski, Tenn. I will leave some things, too, with the hotel keeper for you.

The next morning at 10 o'clock a wagon with a coffin in it drove up to the jail. An officer went into the jail and brought Sam Davis out. He got into the wagon and seated on his coffin was taken to the place of hanging.

Upon reaching the gallows Davis got out of the wagon and took his seat on a bench under a tree. He showed great firmness and glancing at his coffin as it was taken from the wagon, he said, "The boys will have to fight the rest of the battles without me." He asked the officer how long he had to live. He replied, "Fifteen minutes."

The officer said, "I regret very much to have to do this. I feel that I would almost rather die myself than to do what I have to do." Davis replied, "I do not think hard of you; you are doing your duty."

Just at this time another officer approached him and said, "Mr. Davis, I suppose you have not forgotten the offer made you?" Sam, not lifting his head, said, "What is that?" The officer replied, "Your horse and side arms and an escort to the Confederate lines, if you will tell who gave you those papers." To which he replied, "If I had a thousand lives, I would lose them all here and now before I would betray my friends."

The officer then said, "Mr. Davis, I have one more question to ask." Sam said, "What is it?" "I want to know if you are the man my scouts chased last Thursday night, that you crossed the road in front of them, beating their horses in the face with your hat, but got away?" Sam dropped his head and replied, "I have nothing to tell you."

He turned to the officer, saying: "I am ready." Ascending the scaffold, he stepped upon the trap, and without sign of fear or weakness ended a life that was an honor to his family, country, and to the human race.

Only a few years ago, the officer who tied the hangman's knot and sprung the death trap visited the grave of Davis, and with tears in his eyes placed some flowers upon his monument, saying, "He was the best friend I ever had."

The Women of the Confederacy

The "men in gray," the "soldiers behind the guns," were not the only heroes of the great war of the 60's. But the women, the grandmothers of the children of today, were heroic too.

What they did may seem little things to some, but think how you would bear them: hunger, cold, fear, danger, and hard, hard work that you had never dreamed of doing and would not know how to do, anxiety over the loved ones in the war, fighting for "home and mother."

Before a shot was fired at Fort Sumter, Southern women were determined the rights of the South under the Constitution should be maintained even if there should be war. All were open secessionists. They were full of courage, their patriotism ran high. They themselves could not go out and fight, but they sent the men.

The man who failed to announce openly and at once his allegiance to the Southern Confederacy and his intention to fight, was scorned by them and felt their scorn. No Southern belle would allow a young man to visit her who wouldn't enlist; she turned her back upon him, disdainfully plucked aside her skirt when passing him.

Silk dresses were torn up and banners were made out of them, and with smiles and dimples young ladies presented them to the regiments amid cheers, the men waving their hats and the band playing "Dixie."

But soon there was more earnest work for these women. After a big battle the wounded had to be nursed, and how tenderly they did it, and how many homes were turned into hospitals!

Crops had to be raised, and there were only women to see that corn, wheat, and cotton were planted. If the crops failed there would be nothing to eat, and the children and slaves would go hungry, there would be no meal and flour to send to the army and the soldiers would be hungry and faint and could not endure the hardships. So these brave women sent the Negroes to work early every morning and saw to the planting themselves. As long as they had horses they rode all over the country for supplies. They went into the woods themselves to hunt for herbs and roots to make medicines to send to the army, for often the soldiers were sick. In a short time United States gunboats blockaded all Southern ports and stopped or captured all ships trying to get in, so nothing could be brought into the South. Medicines were seized wherever found, there were no drug stores in the South, and the women had to find or make substitutes for the medicines they were accustomed to use.

Large fields of poppies were grown to get opium. Fodder and shuck tea cured chills and fever. To get the much needed quinine, magnolia, and willow bark were stewed down.

In 1863, the soldiers at Vicksburg and in the swamps were shaking with ague and must have quinine. Memphis was then occupied by the Federals and was a kind of a depot of supplies, and of course had plenty of quinine, but the question was how to get it.

It is related that two ladies went from Mississippi to some friends on the outskirts of Memphis and asked their help. They had a passport and sent a pretty young girl of seventeen into the city for the quinine. She went with fear and trembling but determined to get it.

"You can't have it; you are a little old rebel," said the officer at headquarters. She laughed and talked and looked as pretty as she could to win this man's consent.

"Do sell me the quinine; I dare not go home without it," she pleaded.

"You are a rebel; if you will become a Yankee I'll let you have it. Will you take the oath of allegiance?"

She whispered to herself, "I won't take it, I won't, I won't," but that quinine the Confederates must have, what should she do?

"Will you take the oath? Hold up your hand." A man held up her hand, and she shut her eyes and said to herself, "I won't, I won't," while the oath was read to her.

"She is a Union woman now, let her have the quinine," and she got twenty bottles for one hundred dollars, five dollars a bottle. She got other things for her "suffering family," and happy and bright went home. The two ladies were waiting. Hoop skirts were fashionable in those days, and the ladies fastened these bottles of quinine, a pair of boots, flannel shirts, and other things in their hoop skirts and walked out by the Federal soldiers.

Many and many a trip was made in and out of Memphis by ladies and many things did their hoop skirts conceal. This in time became dangerous, because the Federal authorities began to suspect the women and had them searched, and when anything was found on them they were thrown in prison.

Sometimes an appeal for help for the soldiers would come and how those patriotic women would work! "Often at night the hum of the spinning wheel, the scratch, scratch of the cards, the click of the loom could be heard. Every carpet in a little village would be ripped up for saddle blankets for the soldiers; quilts and blankets were made and sent on as fast as willing hands could make them; even curtains were made into shirts; jeans were manufactured into uniforms, and one gallant gentleman in one of these suits of jeans came home on a furlough to be married to the belle and beauty of the county. All this work was done by hands unused to toil, as every Negro was put in the field to make corn and cotton. Pantries were robbed of the last jar of preserves and jelly to send to the hospitals."

When the sky was red with the burning of a house, or word came, "The Federals are coming!" the women secretly buried their jewelry and silver. Many things were buried many times and as many times taken up, but sometimes they could never be found. The children sometimes assisted in this, and how exciting it was that they were actually engaged in burying "sure enough silver" in the dark of the night and maybe someone watching them, ready to shoot at them.

*   *   *   *

After the twin disasters to the Confederacy — Gettysburg and Vicksburg — times were terribly hard in all the Gulf States. Sherman's army was going through the country destroying everything. There was so little to eat, the crops had been destroyed, food and clothing cost so much, and Confederate money was worth so little.

Christmas was at hand and the worried and distressed mothers did not know how Santa Claus was going to fill the children's stockings; it would not do for them to think their patron saint had deserted them entirely, and they wanted the children to have the fun and pleasure they deserved for their good work in helping them.

Little boys, some ten or twelve years old, had scraped lint, or had hid out in the woods and swamps with horses or mules to save them from the enemy; they hunted for rabbits, coons, and possums not only for food but for the skins to make caps for the soldiers. Little girls made bandages, knit socks, and gloves and comforts for the soldiers.

What would the children of today, with expensive mechanical toys and dolls, think, if they got what went into those white home-knit stockings? A baked sweet potato — one of the "big toe" kind — a little box of toilet powder made out of the seeds of the four o'clocks gladdened one girl's heart; a hat made of corn shucks trimmed with plumes fashioned from duck or rooster feathers colored with poke berry juice, indigo and lovejoy; a homespun dress dyed with home-made dyes that smelled strong and rubbed off on the neck and arms — a calico dress, what an extravagance! A little pair of red top boots that cost fourteen dollars went to one little boy, a little bag of shot and one of powder.

The girls gave their mothers Christmas presents of bags of nicely parched wheat if they lived in a wheat country or carefully browned sweet potato strings or little bundles of sassafras roots — all substitutes for coffee, for coffee was an unknown quantity in those troublesome times. Syrup from roughly ground or mashed sugar cane was the only sweetening. Many old ladies drank their coffee without sugar now because they couldn't get sugar "during the war," and so learned to do without it.

Sometimes a courier would ride up and say, "Move out in an hour, General —— (Federal) wants this house for headquarters." Sometimes the order would be, "Move out. You are in the firing line." Hurriedly a few things would be gotten together and they would go to other houses, sometimes they would have to tramp on foot miles out in the country, for they had no horses, the enemy having taken all that had not been sent to the Confederate army. The feet of little children were blistered in the marches and at night they were bathed and the cracks filled with axle grease for there was no vaseline and sweet talcum powder then.

Sometimes houses were seized and used as the Federals pleased; wardrobes of ladies and gentlemen plundered, clothing of whole families taken; pianos, libraries, and ornaments were taken and sent as presents to friends; articles they could never use were many times taken. It was an era of plunder, yet there are many instances of Federal troops showing kindness and consideration.

At Holly Springs, Mississippi, a lady's house was chosen for headquarters for General Grant, but he did not make her move out; he only used what room he needed, shared the dining-room with her and treated her with every courtesy. Afterwards this same lady did not fare so well. Her house was taken for a hospital, and when she refused to go, they were going to move in anyway. An officer told her he would give her a house and helped her and her little children to move; he stayed with them, protected them and watched the house and put out the fires whenever the Federals, who were trying to burn the town, set it on fire. Her house was saved while many others were burned. Months afterwards this officer wrote to this lady's husband, who was in Richmond, to secure his release from Andersonville prison. The husband wrote to the wife about it and she replied, "Get him out if it takes all your time and all your money. For he was my friend in my hour of need."

A white haired friend tells this: "We met a Federal Colonel during the last year of the war who was very kind. My parents were in Atlanta and we were needing some provisions and could not get any. We asked the Colonel to buy us some flour. My sister gave him some silver and sent a Negro with him to bring it. When he came he had a big sack and some sardines and crackers and a package of candy. When we finished eating that candy down at the bottom of that sack we found our same money returned to us."

Love still played its part in the lives of the young people, and many a romance, that ended in marriage, started around the cot of a wounded soldier. The brides sometimes had a hard time getting white wedding dresses. One bride's dress was white tarleton. She had three friends to marry soon after and she lent her dress to them. They in turn sent it to other brides to wear, until finally it disappeared from the neighborhood.

There were pleasures and gayety mixed with their troubles. Sometimes there was a cessation of hostilities and many of the boys in gray came home on furloughs. What preparations the belles made for them. There was sure to be a dance, the gallants dressed in their jeans suits and cowhide boots, the girls in homespun dresses, hair flowing in curls or caught up in nets crocheted at home, and shoes made out of scraps from their fathers' vests, the heels stiffened with leather from dash boards of buggies and carriages, and with soles of home-tanned leather. They did not mind their home-made costumes; they were proud to make sacrifices for "Dixie Land," and danced blithely while the old Negro fiddler would sing out, "Step lightly, Miss Sallie," and call out, "Salute your partners," "Hands all round," "O ladies caper light — Sweetest ladies in de land," while a Negro boy kept time by striking a horse shoe with a nail for the triangle.

The house-servants were busy running across the yard from kitchen to dining-room getting ready the supper, and the windows and doors were filled with the black field hands watching "the White folks" dance, and the old fiddler would make up words to his tunes and sing out the names of his favorites as he swung himself back and forth and sawed away on his fiddle.

The shadows deepened, and the final preparations were made for the last deadly struggle. "For your stricken country's sake and ours," said the "wives, daughters, sisters and friends" of the Confederate soldiers in a published address to them, "be true to yourselves and our glorious cause. Never turn your back on the flag nor desert the ranks of honor or the post of danger. You are constantly present to our minds. The women of the South bestow all their respect and affection on the heroes who defend them."

Sometimes a woman helped a scout on his way and guided him by short ways and little known paths. A horse was furnished one fleeing for his life, another would be concealed and fed until the enemy was gone. Some women gathered information and took it to headquarters; anything, everything to help the beloved cause, and every bit of aid they gave was at the risk of their lives and their homes. With their days and nights running over with sorrow and trouble, the brave women of the South never faltered, never complained, never lost hope, not even when Richmond fell. They bore their part of the dangers and trials of the war uncomplainingly, and when the end came with the same fortitude they took up their changed lives. The men coming home ragged, hatless, faces blanched by want and sickness, most of them tramping footsore, weary, and spent, a few dusty and drooping, home on worn and fagged horses, were consoled and cheered by the women. Many ladies who had been reared in luxury with a large number of servants, went out into their fields and hoed and picked cotton, because, after "freedom come," there were no hands to hire and no money to pay them.

But for the women, the South would have despaired. That the South rose Phoenix-like from the ashes of her cities and towns and wasted fields and broken homes, and is glowing with life and strength, is due to the Women of the Confederacy who fought a good fight and kept the faith.

Mrs. Alexander B. White